How to Land a Strategy Role in Tech

Breaking into BizOps

Amy Sun Yan

ISBN 13: 978-1-63489-572-9

Library of Congress Catalog Number has been applied for.
Printed in the United States of America
First Printing: 2022

26 25 24 23 22 5 4 3 2 1

Cover design by Emily Mahon
Interior design by Patrick Maloney

Wise Ink Creative Publishing
807 Broadway St. NE
Suite 46
Minneapolis, MN 55413

Contents

About the Author

AMY SUN YAN IS currently a strategy and operations program manager at Google, focused on advertiser acquisitions strategy. However, the experiences she writes about in this book are based on her previous role at Google as a strategy and operations analyst. Prior to Google, she worked in BizOps and consulting roles at Facebook (now Meta), Groupon, and McKinsey & Company. Amy grew up in Canton, which is known as the "sweet corn capital" of Michigan. She earned two engineering degrees at Johns Hopkins University, and like 75 percent of the students there, she also dropped out of pre-med.

Outside of work, Amy enjoys mentoring and sharing her learnings. Amy has mentored more than two hundred students through one-on-one calls, speaking series, and office hours, and she has been featured on podcasts such as *Getting Golden* and *10 Minutes of Hiring Wisdom*. Amy's mentees have gone on to work at companies like Google, Amazon, and IBM. These mentoring conversations inspired her to write this book and share her insights so that others could benefit as well.

In 2007, Amy founded a 501(c)(3) nonprofit youth organization called the Little Stars Foundation (thelittlestars.org). She organized young musicians to visit local nursing homes and senior centers to share music and gifts. Amy has served more than a thousand hours on this project, has fundraised $30,000 for the foundation, and continues to serve as board director today.

Amy is also a contributor to Lady Gaga's *New York Times* best-selling book, *Channel Kindness.* She writes about her experience of automating personalized emails to sixteen hundred universities' admissions offices asking for branded T-shirts. After collecting over three thousand items, she then donated these to local high schoolers (targeting first-generation college students) to inspire them to further their education.

Amy currently lives in Mountain View, California, with her husband, Victor, and their mini Australian Shepherd puppy, Roo. In her spare time she loves to pole dance, travel, and play the violin.

Please feel free to reach out and connect with her on LinkedIn (linkedin.com/in/amysunyan).

Acknowledgments

I HAVE TO START by thanking my supportive husband, Victor Yan. From reading early drafts to feeding me while I was editing, he was as important to this book getting finished as I was. Thank you for being an amazing life partner!

Thank you to my parents, Yihong Tong and Kuai-lin Sun, for being constant pillars of support. I'm also immensely grateful to my siblings, Anna and Alan Sun, for inspiring me to continuously push myself.

Next, I want to express my gratitude to Sarah Busby. Thank you for your expertise and time in polishing my manuscript!

Thank you to my Wise Ink Creative Publishing team: Amy Quale, Nyle Vialet, Lauryn Heineman, Emily Mahon, Patrick Maloney, Abbie Phelps, Hanna Kjeldbjerg, Lauren LaGoo, Kari Kasel, and Chelsey Burden. Your collaboration has made my book infinitely better!

Thank you to my friends Jesse Sun, Haylie Chu, Rod Harris-Wright, Jenny Wang, Janice Kim, Erin Twamley, Jamie Xia, and Esther Kim for reviewing early drafts and providing feedback. Thank you to my mentors: Pallavi Shah, Tyler Anderson, Matt Heitz, Sam Mincer, Brandon Kaufmann, Miceh Cumpian, David Bicknell, Deepika Mathur, Eric Lin, Surbhi Nakano, Megha Sharma, Yeon Baik, and Megan Wu. You've taught me the ropes, and I'm very grateful for your time and support.

Last, I owe an enormous debt of gratitude to all my mentees for inspiring me to write this book. Special shout-out to my mentee

Oliver Pour for helping cowrite the chapter on the art of following up. Final thanks go to Jonathan Javier and Jerry Lee (CEO and COO of Wonsulting and ex-Googlers) for connecting me with so many wonderful mentees through their organization! I couldn't have done this without you all.

Foreword

WE CAME ACROSS AMY at the height of the COVID-19 pandemic, in April 2020. At the time, Wonsulting was an infant organization where we mentored more than forty students and early career job seekers to land into Fortune 500 companies. Amy had connected with a number of our mentees and helped provide tangible job tips—they were thrilled. She shared the same passion to help people land their dream jobs as we did, so we got her more involved. She spoke to five thousand aspiring professionals as a guest lecturer during Wonsulting Speaker events and further helped Wonsulting community members in personalized mentorship sessions. Her passion to educate others about her career choices has directly helped her mentees and students to land their dream jobs.

How to Land a Strategy Role in Tech is a terrific read that expands upon the knowledge and strategies presented during Amy's Wonsulting Speaker lectures. Having worked at various tech companies, we feel that the examples provided are clear and concise and truly shed light on the hiring processes we've seen in FAANG companies.

Jonathan Javier, cofounder and CEO at Wonsulting
Jerry Lee, cofounder and COO at Wonsulting

Preface

FINDING A CAREER THAT really taps into your strengths and suits your personality after you've earned your education isn't simple, and there are often bumps along the road. Truly understanding what a job entails and how it might feel, day-to-day, can be quite elusive. It can take time to find that role that fits you like a glove. This is what inspired me to write this book. That insider knowledge was what made the difference in helping me find my path. I wanted to share it to make those first steps that little bit easier. This book is all about the start of your career journey. I often get asked about my story: "How did you transition from college to the workplace?"

Let's go back a few years. I studied biomedical engineering and engineering mechanics at Johns Hopkins University, and I had originally wanted to go into the medical device industry to develop lifesaving and life-improving technologies and devices. However, during my senior year design course, I realized that it would take another five to ten years for our device to get FDA approval and launch in the market. I know myself, and I'm not the most patient person. I wanted to be able to quickly make an impact, so I ultimately decided that the medical device industry was not for me.

Based on suggestions from alumni, I ended up jumping into a consulting role at McKinsey & Company to give myself exposure to different industries and get a better sense of where my interests might lie. In consulting, I seemed to be able to use a lot of the same skills I honed in engineering, such as problem-solving and project management

It was here that I realized I wanted to pursue tech. It's fast-paced, I'm passionate about tech products, and it helps that I use apps like Facebook and Instagram every day. I spent some time in the banking industry, creating benchmarks and coming up with repricing strategies, which only made my choice clearer. When clients talked about "wire transfers," my eyes would just glaze over, as I had never sent or received a wire myself. Meanwhile, when I think about changing a button from green to red on my Facebook feed, that's very tangible to me, and I understand it from a user perspective.

However, I found external consulting frustrating, as you're only able to work on creating the strategy and not the implementation. Often, I would follow up with a client, and they would say they "didn't have the resources" or "couldn't get the headcount" to implement my recommendations. This would be really unsatisfying. It felt like I'd wasted my effort, and I didn't see anything come to fruition.

Now that I've transitioned into internal consulting in tech, I feel much more fulfilled because I get to work end-to-end on both the strategy *and* the execution of a decision. Also, because I'm an employee within the company, I can get a much closer perspective on what's happening day to day, and I can more easily build personal relationships with my stakeholders and "clients." I'm currently working at Google in the strategy and operations team within the sales organization, and most of my work involves coming up with strategies to acquire, onboard, and sustain new advertisers who've never used Google before. I find this type of work rewarding because I will help fundamentally shape the direction of the company over the next few years.

It hasn't all been plain sailing, though. Coming from an engineering background and going into business, I faced challenges, including ramping up on Excel, strengthening presentation skills, and understanding business jargon. It took a little longer for me to learn since I hadn't taken any of these courses in school, but I eventually got there and was able to perform just as well as anyone else. If you're interested in a field that you didn't study, don't be discouraged! I was able to make the transition, and you'll be able to as well.

At the height of the COVID-19 pandemic in April 2020, I came across Wonsulting while researching potential mentorship programs for professional development.

Wonsulting is an organization that helps job seekers from non-traditional backgrounds (e.g., non-target schools, first-generation) land their dream careers. The cofounders, Jonathan Javier and Jerry Lee, come from strategy and operations backgrounds from top companies including Google, Snap, Cisco, and Lucid Software. So far, they've helped tens of thousands receive offers and have been featured on Forbes, Newsweek, and Business Insider. Through Wonsulting, I got introduced to many of my mentees, and these conversations inspired me to share the major insights and takeaways in this book.

So, that was my journey. I feel I've found where I can thrive. It took time to see what combination worked for me, but that learning process ultimately led me toward a more tailor-made career path. I hope this book helps you to do the same.

PART ONE

Looking for a Job in BizOps

1

What Is Business Operations (BizOps)?

WHEN I TELL SOMEONE that I work in business operations (colloquially referred to as BizOps), nine times out of ten the reaction is "What is that?" Over the last few decades, many businesses have developed teams that look internally in an effort to self-improve. Historically, this kind of work has been done by external consulting firms, but it's increasingly being brought in-house because it's cheaper, more flexible, and more efficient.

I like to think of BizOps as a company's internal consulting agency. Whenever there are important strategic questions or high-priority initiatives, the BizOps team is brought in to crack the case. Typically, BizOps teams are composed of former bankers and consultants with strong spreadsheet and presentation skills.

The major difference between BizOps and external consultants is that consultants are only involved with making recommendations and move on to the next project before seeing results. For most external consultants, the output is almost always analytical. For example, they might suggest a series of cost-cutting recommendations rather than outlining how to implement them. As mentioned previously, the BizOps team is responsible for both recommendations *and* execution. The output is therefore action-oriented instead of just analytical: they enact real change, on the ground. In the BizOps team, you're no longer just the analyst; you're also the operator. You need to make decisions and get things done, often with limited information and resources at your disposal.

So, what's a typical day for a BizOps professional? The short answer is there isn't one! You may be analyzing data, developing SQL and Python skills, writing up a strategic business plan, designing and monitoring pilot projects, interviewing candidates, setting up and monitoring key performance indicators (KPIs), drafting best-practice playbooks for sellers, or building dashboards. BizOps roles can vary widely by company and team, so it's important to read the job description carefully and meet with members of the team to understand the day-to-day work they normally undertake.

In many companies, there's a centralized BizOps team. This way, team members stay focused on the company as a whole and can remain more objective than if they were reporting directly to the manager they're advising. From my experience, a centralized BizOps team works well. It helps members share learnings across different functions and ensures that work isn't being duplicated across teams.

Last, it's worth noting that there's a huge variation in job titles for the BizOps role and their department names, which could impact your research and job search. Below is a list of the various job titles that you may encounter that are synonymous with or similar to BizOps professional:

- Business operations specialist
- Business analyst
- Business operations manager
- Business strategist
- Strategy operations analyst

- Internal consultant
- Tech strategist
- Corporate strategy associate
- Operations associate (e.g., sales, product, market, legal)

You will see this in action in my description of roles at various companies in chapter 2.

Who Do BizOps Teams Recruit and Attract?

BizOps and strategy teams tend to recruit from certain roles that have transferable skills and relevance to their mission. These ideal roles are generally the following:

- Product and corporate strategy teams across the industry (e.g., at Netflix, Airbnb, Uber)
- Consultants, ideally in tech, economics, and/or with an engineering or science background (e.g., Cornerstone Research)
- Product managers (PMs) who are interested in broader strategic work rather than individual projects
- Data science (DS) specialists and similar roles with an analytical function who are interested in moving away from individual products and toward a horizontal "ecosystem" approach

As you might expect, the above roles prepare you well for BizOps, but the flexibility goes both ways. BizOps also prepares you well for the roles listed above, and if you feel you want a change after a few years, you can pursue another avenue based on what motivated you most in your role. For example, if you think, "I want to go deeper into analytics," there is data science; if you think, "I love the deal process," there's corporate development and strategy; if you think, "I want to build," there is product management.

Whom Will I Work Most Closely with on a Day-to-Day Basis?

Our role is highly cross functional, which means that interpersonal skills are important to have and develop. Typically, bringing people together from different disciplines can improve problem-solving and lead to more thorough decision-making. Our day-to-day involves close partnership across a number of teams within the company, including product managers, product marketing managers (PMMs), project managers, program managers, engineers, and data scientists.

Let's look at the responsibilities of some of these teams. Product managers are responsible for making sure that a team delivers a great product. Product marketing managers work to find product-market fit and develop the go-to-market strategy and external communications. Project managers are responsible for breaking down a large-scale project into manageable chunks. They'll coordinate, estimating the timelines of the project and making sure things stay on track. Program managers oversee a group of dependent projects that help reach the program goals. They lead the program strategy and objectives and assess the business impact. Engineers are the bread and butter of any tech company, and they're responsible for building the product from the ground up. Data scientists run A/B tests and analyze results, and they help build dashboards to track metrics.

Product manager, program manager, and project manager can all be abbreviated as PM, and many people confuse the terms. I've created the definitions above from my own experience and hope they're helpful for you, but keep in mind that these titles can mean different things at different companies so, again, it's worth clarifying with the team.

What Is Covered in This Book?

This book provides a comprehensive overview of landing a strategy role in a tech company. You'll learn how the role varies across companies, what experience is needed to land this type of role, and what a great resume and cover letter look like. Finally, it covers how to master the interview and tackle question types, including general, behavioral, case, technical, and take-home. You'll find clear and specific examples and practice problems throughout. We'll also go beyond interview guidance and talk through how to network, get a referral, and write a resume, as well as tips to succeed after you land the role.

This book is broken down into three parts for easy navigation: pre-interview, interview, and post-interview:

Part 1: Looking for a Job in BizOps

Part 2: The BizOps Interview

Part 3: Landing the Job in BizOps

I've worked with countless current and aspiring BizOps analysts to help them learn how to get the right experience, how to position themselves appropriately, how to prepare for interviews, and how to ace them. This book translates these many hours of coaching sessions and conversations into written form.

And, finally, a quick disclaimer for the rest of the book: the opinions stated here are my own and not those of my company or any of the companies I've worked with.

2

Choosing the Right Company

ONE OF THE BIGGEST questions in a BizOps candidate's mind is "What's the difference between all these companies?" When you are trying to work out where to apply to and how to tailor your application, this is important. While the BizOps role may sound similar at many companies, in practice there can be a big difference in what day-to-day life is like.

Company attitudes on factors like transparency between divisions and work-life balance vary. The BizOps role also varies in scope and in terms of how much of the job involves data analysis, oral and written communication, strategy, and project management.

Since I've worked at Google, Facebook, and Groupon, I can directly compare the three companies and tell you what the BizOps role is like at each. This should give you insight into this role at big and midsize tech companies.

At Google, there are multiple different teams with some variation of "business operations and strategy" in their titles, all focused on different areas of the business. There are global and regional strategy teams focused on sales, another focused on enterprise, and additional teams for partnerships, just to name a few. Therefore, BizOps roles are a little less clear-cut, and you'll need to look at the job description carefully to determine the scope. However, this does mean there are many more opportunities to work in this area than at Facebook.

There is a central BizOps team, however, and it functions like an internal consulting arm for Google VPs. It largely works on special projects for VPs and strategic deep dives of different areas of the business.

The team that I'm working in, strategy and operations (StratOps), is larger than the central BizOps team and actually falls under the sales organization. In terms of our day-to-day purpose and activities, we support our business partners (e.g., cross-functional teams like marketing) by being internal consultants and chiefs of staff. We help define and execute the goal that's outlined by the leadership team. For example, the goal for the organization may be to double revenue in the next five years. In order to break this down, we'll focus on initiatives such as strengthening the customer journey, revamping sales team structures, or redesigning marketing incentives. We'll then deep dive into one of these areas. Let's take marketing incentives as an example. We'll start by doing customer research and diving into the data to figure out the answers to questions like, "Who should get incentives? What kind of incentives should we offer (e.g., rewards, coupons, freebies, etc.)? When should we offer these incentives? Do higher or lower value incentives lead to higher ROI?"

We also support various initiatives, often in roles that are a mix of program/project management, consulting, and analysis.

Our team's background varies depending on the team and product they are supporting, but the majority of people have a background in either consulting (think McKinsey, Boston Consulting Group) or investment banking, and they usually have strong financial modeling and quantitative analysis skills.

Google assesses candidates based on four attributes:

1. **Role-related knowledge:** This includes work proficiency and history as well as rate of advancement.

2. **Leadership:** This includes influence/impact, motivating others, and taking initiative.

3. **General cognitive ability (GCA):** This includes analytical ability, strategic thinking, and intellectual curiosity.

4. **Googleyness:** This includes ambition/drive, collaboration and interpersonal skills, bias to action, thriving in ambiguity, challenging the status quo, valuing feedback, making ethical decisions, and caring about the team.

These four attributes are designed to allow interviewers to evaluate candidates in a clear, consistent manner as relevant to the role. The weighting of these attributes may vary depending on the actual requirements for the role. For example, the leadership expectations for a people manager may be different than for an individual contributor.

The third bucket, general cognitive ability (GCA), is *not* related to grades (GPA), where a candidate attended school, or what their standardized test scores were. While these attributes may be evidence of GCA, interviewers are instructed not to make assumptions about a candidate's GCA based on them. Instead, interviewers will use specific questions to assess GCA as it relates to the role in the interview process.

I've heard some interviewees say, "I thought Googleyness was the incredible things that candidates do outside of work, like volunteering at a nonprofit, running a marathon, being an accomplished violinist, or competing in the Olympics."

In actuality, Googleyness is a set of behaviors that influence whether someone will be successful at Google—those that tend to be related to their ability to thrive in Google's environment. For some candidates, it's easy to see how activities outside of work demonstrate Googleyness: a marathon may demonstrate ambition and bias to action, for example. However, many successful candidates (especially those experienced hires who aren't new graduates) will also be able to demonstrate these behaviors through their prior work experience.

Facebook (now known as Meta)

Please note that I was at Facebook before it was renamed to Meta, so I will refer to the company as "Facebook" when I talk about my own experiences. At Facebook, BizOps falls under the finance organization.

When I was at Facebook, our BizOps team worked closely with product groups on the strategic direction of our investments (e.g., Should we invest more employee headcount into Facebook Marketplace since we think e-commerce will take off?). Our team was responsible for revenue forecasting and would come up with dollar projections for the next six months or next few years. This involved projecting out based on past performance using Prophet, an open-source forecasting tool in Python or R, and then taking out one-time events like elections, holidays, and large product changes.

Once we created these projections (known as pulling forward the "organic" curve because it represents the organic growth of the company without any changes to the product), we worked with product managers to understand what changes they had planned so we could add those on top of the organic forecast.

Finally, we collaborated with data science partners, looking at A/B tests to understand the magnitude of these product enhancements to metrics like revenue and engagement (e.g., time spent, sessions, etc.).

In case you're not familiar with the term "A/B testing," it is an experimentation method that allows you to test two variants (red button versus green button) on a small population before deciding which one is better to roll out to the broader population. For example, we added a "care" emoji and showed it to 10 percent of the population to see if it got positive reactions. Since it was received well, we ended up rolling it out to 100 percent of users. We rely on data from A/B tests to help us understand growth, optimize for user satisfaction, and increase revenue.

At Facebook, each analyst is assigned an area of monetization—a section of the business that generates income. For example, my responsibility was forecasting revenue for Facebook Newsfeed, while other analysts were creating revenue projections for IG Stories, IG Feed, WhatsApp, Messenger, Marketplace, and so on. We combined these forecasts to produce an overall picture of growth at Facebook and presented the results to the VPs of analytics, product, and finance. Finally, the presentations were distilled and shared with the CFO, COO, and CEO.

Our forecasts showed leadership the outlook for our portfolio of investments and gave them ideas for the best areas to invest in next. Where should we make our next big bet—commerce, video, AR/VR, or gaming? Those were the types of questions we would help answer. In addition, our forecasts would help with resource allocation and deciding where to put the next hundred engineering hires.

Outside of forecasting cycles, we also helped out with quarterly earnings reports. This is when, each quarter, Facebook announces how they performed compared to analysts' expectations and what their outlook is for the next quarter. Every month, my team prepped our CFO with the latest revenue and engagement trends. We would also update him on any new product launches, and he would ask us for sound bites to use when presenting this information to investors. Even as an analyst, I got the opportunity to present to the CFO, which was awesome! It's rare to get such a high-visibility role as an analyst, the bottom level of the corporate ladder, but with BizOps it is possible.

Work-life balance is heavily dependent on the manager. One of my managers was very detail-oriented and wanted to have every slice of the data available in the appendix in case a question popped up about it. That led to many long nights of working on fifty-page appendices that weren't necessarily even brought up in meetings. When I switched managers (but stayed on the same team), I had a completely different experience with work-life balance. Most days I was in the office from 9:30 a.m. to 5:30 p.m. and finished up all my work with no issues. Since work-life balance is very team- and manager-dependent, I recommend having honest conversations with other members of the team to understand exactly what you're signing up for.

For me, the only downside of being a BizOps analyst at Facebook was that more than 40 percent of my time was spent working on operational tasks (e.g., Excel modeling) as opposed to more strategic projects (e.g., How should we price the new Oculus product?). We repeated forecasting cycles four times a year. After six cycles of forecasting, I felt I'd exhausted the available learning opportunities.

When you feel like you hit that point, you have one of three options: you can stay in the same team and expand your current scope (for example, I was working on a mature product called Newsfeed and wanted to expand to a newer product like Facebook Stories), switch companies, or make a lateral move at your current company.

The internal transfer process at Facebook is pretty straightforward. You need one year of experience in your current role and manager approval. During my time at Facebook, other team members had no problem having the conversation with our manager and happily switched into other roles in product marketing, product management, or sales operations.

Groupon

Groupon is an e-commerce marketplace that connects users with local merchants offering activities, travel, goods, and services at a discount. Unlike Google and Facebook, Groupon is not headquartered in the Bay Area but rather in Chicago, Illinois.

At Groupon, the BizOps team fell under the product organization. We served primarily as product analysts, supporting the product manager (PM) teams and helping them use data to drive decisions for their roadmaps. For example, one of my projects involved redesigning the search bar to make it easier for users to convert into purchasers. After a few months, I was promoted to lead international analyst, and my primary project was closing the gap in revenue per user between the US and the rest of the world. I got the opportunity to go on my first international business trip to London and Dublin and meet the sales and marketing teams based in those offices.

Since Groupon was a smaller company (two thousand employees at HQ and six thousand employees overall during my time), I felt like I had a chance to wear many hats. I took on data automation projects and dashboard-building projects that would usually fit a data scientist or data engineer role. I took on product manager projects to recommend new features and worked with engineers and designers to bring those to life. I also interviewed candidates and helped with grading the take-home challenges.

The other benefit of a smaller company is the consistent exposure to senior leaders. Even though I had less than two years of professional experience when I joined, I immediately had the responsibility of creating weekly business reports that went directly to the CFO.

The downside to a smaller company is that it can be unstable. The stock price for Groupon could fluctuate more than 30 percent in one day. Since equity can be a large portion of your compensation, this is worth taking into account when deciding on your next company. Many of my coworkers were furloughed during the COVID-19 pandemic. Even before that, entire offices, including those in the Bay Area and Seattle, were closed, and workers were relocated to the headquarters in Chicago. These types of events can happen, and although they are unlikely, they are something you should keep in mind.

3

Getting the Right Experience

USUALLY, WHEN YOU ASK interviewers what they're looking for in BizOps candidates, they'll say they are looking for smart, passionate people who can get stuff done.

These attributes will be reflected in the job descriptions for BizOps or strategy and operations job openings. So, what does this mean in real terms? While the actual list of requirements will be more comprehensive, it will ultimately boil down to two criteria:

1. Can you be trusted to make the right decisions?
2. Can you push through potential roadblocks to deliver great results to your clients?

You'll want to focus on these two criteria when you think about the kinds of experience you want to acquire. For example, whenever possible, see your projects through to the end. Focus on what you did and the outcomes of your actions. If your outcomes were successful, consider why they were successful and by what metrics you've defined success. If your outcomes weren't successful, that's also okay, but understand the reason you failed. This will help you to reflect on the skills you already have and the ones you need to work on. You'll also need to be able to discuss these experiences at your interview.

Let's look in more detail at the experience you need and how to acquire it. First, I'll look at the opportunity to break into BizOps as a new graduate and how to stand out in the crowd. Then I'll explore LinkedIn and career fairs as tools to get your foot in the door and expand your network.

Can I Get into BizOps as a New Graduate?

Business operations is a great role to get into right out of college. Many big companies have university recruiting programs and pride themselves on training new graduates to become top-notch business operations professionals.

For example, Meta has its Finance & Business Operations Analyst Rotation Program, which opens up applications in June or July every year. In this role, new graduates have the unique opportunity to gain invaluable experience across a broad range of functions and create a large impact in a growing finance organization. Successful candidates for this team tend to be well-rounded top performers who want to build a strong finance background and who can contribute in a high-intensity growth environment.

LinkedIn has something similar called the Strategy & Analytics (S&A) Program, "a two-year rotational program designed as a career accelerator that prepares new college graduates to become exceptional business leaders. In high-visibility roles, S&A analysts master business skills such as strategic framing, SQL & Presto, financial modeling, data visualization, and performance management. The S&A program also provides learning and development workshops and both executive and peer mentoring."[1]

If you're a student and want to improve your chances of getting hired into these or similar rotational programs, consider doing the following:

- **Take group project courses.** This will demonstrate that you can hit the ground running in a team environment.

1 "LinkedIn Strategy & Analytics," LinkedIn Careers, accessed February 6, 2021, https://careers.linkedin.com/students/strategy-and-analytics.

- **Take on a leadership role.** This can be anything from sports team captain to class president. As a BizOps analyst, you'll need strong leadership skills to convince stakeholders of your ideas and to create actionable impact.

- **Participate in case competitions.** Case competitions are extracurricular events where students compete to develop the best solution to a business problem (based on a case study). Case competitions are a great way for you to get exposure to consulting cases, which are a major component of the business operations interview. The additional benefit is that you get the opportunity to present to an audience of industry professionals, which is beneficial for networking down the line. If you win, there could be monetary prizes as well!

- **Start a side project.** One of the best ways to rise above the crowd is to start a side project like a mobile app. This gives you a chance to show your technical skills and customer focus. If you don't have the technical skills to do this on your own, partner with a friend who can help you do some of the building.

- **Intern as a business operations analyst, finance analyst, data scientist, or product manager.** There's nothing better than learning on the job, and an internship gives you that chance. It might also result in an opportunity to convert to a full-time role in that company.

The key thing is to show something beyond your coursework to an interviewer. Find a way to demonstrate your initiative, your leadership and business skills, and your technical prowess.

Making the Most of Career Fairs

Career fairs can be a great way for you to get your foot in the door, especially at smaller companies. You'll find both big and small companies at career fairs, but smaller companies tend to put more stock into this method of finding candidates and don't have the resources to compete with larger organizations on other fronts (like social media and marketing to reach out to students). When you chat with professionals at the career fair booth and hand over your resume, they'll make some notes about the impression you made. These notes can mean the difference between getting an interview or having your resume ignored.

Here are some tips for how to make the best impression with potential employers and use your time wisely:

Research which companies will be at the career fair and decide which ones you're most interested in. Then check if they have strategy-related roles available. If you have a priority list of employers to approach and know which ones are most relevant to you, you can spend your time on the most valuable opportunities.

Choose your words carefully for your introduction and elevator pitch. Think about what makes you stand out and what makes you look like a great candidate to them. Perhaps it's the challenging class project you led, or maybe you've done something to show initiative such as starting a debating club. These would be great things to discuss.

Practice your introduction and pitch in front of a mirror, or better yet, record yourself on video. Trust me, you will be your own harshest critic! Just keep practicing how you'll walk up to the booth, introduce yourself, and talk about your accomplishments without feeling awkward.

Have some questions in your back pocket. Ask questions that can only be answered by current employees and not by a simple online search. This lets them know you've done your research. The types of questions you ask will also reveal more about your values. This is a subtle way of telling them that you are a good fit for their culture.

Pay attention to the crowds at the booths. Consider approaching those that have less footfall. This could be a great time to get to know a smaller company that you might not have thought of before. If their booth isn't busy, the volunteers will likely be more willing to chat longer with you and make a real connection. You won't just be white noise in the crowd.

Don't just hand over your resume without talking to people at the booth first. If you do that, you'll be missing out on the unique benefits of being able to interact with company employees firsthand. They will also be more likely to forget you if you make no impression at all.

While it's important to be professional, don't be afraid to be a little different! It's good to show some personality and passion so that you stand out as an individual who has something new to offer them. For example, if you've built something cool, feel free to show the booth volunteers some pictures or a demo video on your phone. This will also help them remember you.

Making the Most of LinkedIn

Despite being professionals, few of us spend much time thinking about our LinkedIn profile. You may not think it's worth it, but in reality, LinkedIn offers a wealth of opportunity, and engaging on the platform regularly can have a positive impact on your career. "With more than 55 million companies listed on the site and 14 million open jobs, it's not a surprise that 87 percent of recruiters regularly use LinkedIn," writes Maddy Osman for Kinsta.[2] It's one of the best untapped resources for job-searching content (e.g.,

2 Maddy Osman, "Mind-Blowing LinkedIn Statistics and Facts (2021)," Kinsta, May 11, 2021, https://kinsta.com/blog/linkedin-statistics/.

application tips, industry news, and job announcement posts) and connections online, so if there were ever a time to get back on your profile, this would be it!

Finding New Connections and Job Opportunities

Jobs are posted on LinkedIn all the time, but there are subtler ways of making connections with recruiters and finding opportunities before they are even made public. One way you can take advantage of LinkedIn is to search for "I'm happy to announce . . ." posts in the search bar and filter to "All post results." You're probably familiar with this type of post:

I'm happy to announce I'll be working at Meta.

I'm happy to announce I'll be interning at Amazon.

Instead of getting jealous of others' accomplishments, you can turn their "I'm happy to announce . . ." posts into an opportunity and get your foot in the door with top companies by doing the following:

Scroll to the bottom of the posts and see if they have a "thank you" section where they tag a list of people who have helped them throughout the recruiting process. You'll notice that most of those tagged people are hiring managers or recruiters for specific positions. Reach out to those same people and mention that you would love to learn about more opportunities and receive guidance from them as well! This way, you'll be at the forefront of their minds when new job openings pop up, and they can easily reach out to you.[3]

3 Jonathan Javier, "How to Change an 'I'm Happy to Announce . . .' Post into Your Own," LinkedIn, November 18, 2019, https://www.linkedin.com/pulse/how-change-im-happy-announce-post-your-own-jonathan-javier/?trackingId=S11mB2VITXq49kQqdjf%2Bcw%3D%3D.

Using Your Existing Network

Another underutilized resource is your current network! Many people think that networking just means talking to strangers, but there are so many opportunities that can come from tapping into your existing relationships or contacts.

Luckily, LinkedIn makes this very easy to do. Click on "My Network" and "Connections" to view your current first-degree connections. You can filter them down to their current company and location pretty easily as well.

If you're looking for a role at Google in the Bay Area, simply set the filters to get the list of current connections you should reach out to.

Another tip: if you're reaching out, make sure to send messages from Monday to Friday. Those sent during the working week are more likely to be responded to than those sent out on the weekend!

Cold Messaging Industry Professionals

A cold call is an unsolicited call to an employer to attempt to schedule a meeting or job interview with them. It can be nerve-racking to pick up the phone to call someone you don't know and ask them about job openings, but it works. Nowadays, people don't often use calls but instead will utilize cold messaging.

When you cold message professionals and hiring managers on LinkedIn, make sure you do the following to minimize your chances of getting ignored, advises Wonsulting cofounder Jerry Lee.[4] In my connection requests, only about 30 percent of people

---

4 Jerry Lee, "When You Cold Message Recruiters & Hiring Managers on LinkedIn," LinkedIn post, accessed January 30, 2021, https://www.linkedin.com/posts/jehakjerrylee_justjerry-studentvoices-activity-6651355673504337920-PISa.

will add a personalized invite and even fewer will tailor the message.

Tip 1: When you send a connection request, use a personalized message.

When inviting members to connect, you can add a personalized message to the recipient to introduce yourself or add context to your relationship. This will single-handedly make you stand out, and it doesn't require you to pay for a LinkedIn Premium account.

Tip 2: Tailor your message to the individual.

To further increase your chances, spend one or two minutes looking through the person's profile, and incorporate what you learn into your message. I've had students ask me about the nonprofit organization I started, and that always leads to a good conversation!

Tip 3: Make sure to follow up.

Most people are busy! Silence isn't always a sign that they are ignoring you. If someone doesn't reply, then make sure to follow up in a week to give them a gentle reminder.

Cold Messaging Recruiters

A job has been posted and you want to apply, but the recruiter won't get back to your request. The reason why you're not getting replies is probably because you're not tailoring messages to the job they're hiring for.

One of the easiest things you can do to increase your chances of recruitment into tech companies is to use the job description and structure the message accordingly. There should be one sentence explaining why you're interested in the role, one sentence showing you meet the minimum requirements, and two to three bullets showing you have the preferred qualifications.

Below is an example of a Meta business operations analyst job posting:

> Meta's mission is to give people the power to build community and bring the world closer together. Through our family of apps and services, we're building a different kind of company that connects billions of people around the world, gives them ways to share what matters most to them, and helps bring people closer together. Whether we're creating new products or helping a small business expand its reach, people at Meta are builders at heart. Our global teams are constantly iterating, solving problems, and working together to empower people around the world to build community and connect in meaningful ways. Together, we can help people build stronger communities—we're just getting started. This is a highly cross-functional role, involving close partnership across a number of teams within Meta, including PM, PMM, Engineering, Data Science, Product Strategy, Operations, and Partnerships teams. Responsibilities will include driving revenue forecasting and planning, developing operational insights for the business, and modeling business scenarios to guide product decisions. This team focuses on analysis and data-driven decision-making, which allows us to work effectively with our colleagues in the rest of the business in order to optimize long-term financial growth. Successful candidates will have exceptional analytical skills, a bias toward action, exceptional partnering and communication skills, and strong interest in the internet/tech media ecosystem.

DESCRIPTION

Responsibilities

- Build revenue forecasts, analyze current business performance, and assess market opportunities
- Develop and track operational and financial metrics
- Lead and coordinate cross-functional strategic projects
- Present outcomes at reviews with business leaders across Meta
- Develop high-trust partnerships across a number of product-facing teams

Minimum Qualifications

- 3+ years of experience in consulting, investment banking, business strategy, business operations, or analytics
- Experience synthesizing strategic insights and problem-solving individually or in a group setting
- Experience using Microsoft Excel

Preferred Qualifications

- BA/BS in engineering, computer science, math, economics, statistics, or other quantitative field
- Experience using SQL and R

Here's a sample message to a recruiter for this job posting:

Hi Sam,

Thanks for connecting! I have been following your blog and I saw that you recruit for Meta here in the Bay Area. My name is Ashley and I'm interested in applying for the Business Operations Analyst role at Meta. With three years of experience in consulting and operations roles, I'm confident I'd be a great fit for this role. In my current role at Groupon, I recently launched a new product feature, and we've seen 10 percent increases in key operational metrics as a result.

Do you have a few minutes to chat this week? I'd welcome the opportunity to learn more about the role and share how my skills and experiences would benefit the team. I've also attached my resume in case that is helpful!

Thanks,

Ashley

If, on the other hand, a recruiter reached out to you for an open role, here's a good sample response if you're interested in the opportunity:

Hi Lisa,

Thanks for reaching out! The position you mentioned sounds interesting, and I'd love to talk and hear more about it. I'm free Wednesday through Friday from 10:00 a.m. to 4:00 p.m. EST this week and my number is 666-666-6666.

Please let me know what date/time works best for you!

Best regards,

David

If it's an opportunity you're not interested in, I still recommend you send a note to establish a relationship with the recruiter. Even if it's not a fit right now, you may begin searching for roles later on and you'll be able to return to this message to re-engage the recruiter. Here's a sample response to illustrate how you might do this:

> Hi Charles,
>
> Thanks for reaching out! While this position seems interesting, I'm really happy where I'm at right now. With that said, if I'm looking to make a change in the future, I'll make sure to reach out. Thanks again and good luck filling the position!
>
> Best,
>
> Dustin

Do I Need an MBA?

I've thought about this question quite a bit. I myself have taken GMAT prep classes and the GMAT itself, which prepares you for admission to graduate business programs. However, later on I decided that it wasn't worth doing an MBA. This is a very personal decision, though, and I think the answer really depends on your situation.

If you're considering an MBA, here are some questions to help you think through your decision. I've included my own thought process, as this might help you to analyze your current position and whether it will benefit you.

What Is an MBA Useful For?

An MBA is useful for helping you find the right career path, land a higher-level position or salary, network, or fill in coursework gaps if you studied something completely different at an undergraduate level. Let's look at these in a little more detail.

Finding the right career path: For those that want to explore a different career path, an MBA could be a great idea. An MBA would (1) help supplement any coursework that you might be missing from your undergraduate experience, (2) give you the opportunity to build your network, and (3) allow you to try a summer internship in this new career path to make the full-time transition easier. For example, you might be interested in transitioning from English teacher to an entirely new field, such as private equity. The MBA will allow you to take finance courses and find the connections to better prepare you for the private equity track.

Improving your level and salary: The pay for those with an MBA is considerably higher than for many other jobs in business. One of my friends was an executive assistant before her MBA and held typical "secretary" and "assistant" roles. After getting her MBA, she landed a marketing manager role at a manufacturing company and doubled her salary within her first year of graduating.

Networking: An MBA helps you build a professional network and is one of the most important factors for many students. The other students you'll meet will likely end up being business partners or giving you referrals to your dream company down the line. You'll also be able to reach out to alumni to shadow and learn more about their day-to-day roles.

Coursework: Core courses in an MBA program include various areas, such as accounting, applied statistics, business communication, finance, management, marketing, and operations management. If you were a history major in college but wanted to make the switch to investment banking, an MBA could help you fill those coursework gaps you needed to make that transition.

What Does an MBA Cost?

As someone who is interested in business, it's important for me to understand the return on investment (ROI) for business school. ROI = return (benefit) / investment (cost). Now that we've gone over some of the benefits, let's turn to the costs.

The first and most obvious cost is money. If you take into account tuition, living expenses, and books, a two-year on-campus MBA can cost between $100,000 and $200,000. If you don't have that money available, you'll likely need to take on financial aid or loans. Keep in mind that, if you graduate with considerable debt, you'll need to make enough money to cover your loans as well as living expenses.

On average, MBAs who graduated from Harvard Business School in 2020 make a $150,000 median base salary after graduation.[5] However, if you decide to go down the startup route and create a business from scratch, you could be making much less for several years.

Another large cost of an MBA is time. Two years is a lot of time that you could've spent mastering a skill, gaining relevant experience, or starting your own venture.

These are all factors that you should consider, but ultimately,

5 "Employment Data," Harvard Business School, accessed June 30, 2020, https://www.hbs.edu/recruiting/data/Pages/at-a-glance.aspx.

the choice to do an MBA is very dependent on your situation and what you're looking to get out of it.

Why I Decided an MBA Doesn't Make Sense for Me

Let's go back to the benefits of an MBA. I considered each of these in turn in relation to my current position.

> **Finding the right career path:** I'm pretty sure that I want to continue in the strategy and operations space. Since I'm not planning to make a huge career switch, I don't think an MBA is required.
>
> **Improving your level and salary:** In my current position, I'm a level-five strategy and operations program manager at Google with six years of work experience. Most MBAs come into Google at level four to five, so a two-year MBA wouldn't help fast-track my career at this point. My current base salary is also close to a Harvard MBA's median base salary after graduation. So, financially, it wouldn't make sense for me to do an MBA now.
>
> **Networking:** It's true that your MBA network will include potential clients and deals as well as classmates who can teach you about new industries. However, I have been very proactive about networking at my current and previous companies, so I have a good foundation there already. I think that if you are proactive, you can build a comparable network while working instead of doing an MBA.
>
> **Coursework:** Similarly, I'm able to continue closing the gap in my coursework while in my current role. I studied biomedical engineering in college, so I never took any courses in finance or data science. Since it's useful to have a baseline knowledge in those subjects, I've been actively com-

pleting Google's internal training programs and external coursework. My favorite course so far has been Stanford's Continuing Studies STAT 05 W, Statistics for Artificial Intelligence, Machine Learning, and Data Science. However, there are many other options out there for improving your knowledge base, some of which I've listed next.

Alternatives to an MBA

An MBA isn't the only way for you to make progress in your career. There are many other options. Consider the following and whether they better suit you and your current circumstances:

Start from the bottom and work your way up the corporate ladder: Get an entry-level job or internship at the company you want to join (or a similar company within the same industry) and work your way up. It may take a while to get what you want, but you'll at least have the opportunity to grow with the company and see where the position takes you. For example, my friend Ellen started as an account strategist at Google right after graduating. She moved up to account executive and then finally transitioned to her dream role of global business strategy associate.

Get a technical master's degree: Degrees in subjects like computer science and human-computer interaction are common in tech companies, but from what I've seen, those degrees are more useful for roles in data science, engineering, or UX design. If you're interested in pivoting to one of those roles rather than BizOps, it makes more sense to pursue a technical master's degree than an MBA. While you'll learn different skills than those taught in business school, the time commitments and costs are similar.

Try a bootcamp: Bootcamps are comprehensive but condensed learning programs that are designed to teach practical skills of a certain discipline. There are programs like Hack Reactor or Tradecraft that are designed for closing skill gaps in coding, design, or marketing. For example, if you want to go from a BizOps role to product management (where you're working with a team of engineers), you could get there by (1) internally switching teams at your current company, (2) doing a technical bootcamp to get more coding experience on your resume, or (3) getting an MBA. While bootcamps can range quite a bit, they usually cost between $5,000 and $15,000 and take twelve to fourteen weeks. Bootcamps do cost less in terms of money and time, but they offer fewer options than an MBA because they're often not accredited and do not have the same name recognition.

Shadow someone: This is a cross between a formal internship and a do-it-yourself option. Shadowing is essentially observing an experienced professional so you can better understand the day-to-day role and decide if it's the right career path for you.

Teach yourself: There's a huge amount of free and low-cost learning content on the internet. If you have the time and discipline to create your own curriculum, this is always an option. I've listed just a few of the many resources available here:

1. Forage (formerly InsideSherpa) "is an open access platform designed to unlock exciting careers for students by connecting them to company endorsed Virtual Intern

programs" from Boston Consulting Group, Deloitte, JP-Morgan Chase, KPMG, Accenture, and many others.[6]

2. MIT OpenCourseWare is a web-based publication of virtually all MIT course content for free!

3. Coursera partners with 150 universities to offer thousands of free and paid courses. You can even receive certificates and show them off when you finish a course! [7]

4. Some other great options include Udemy, LinkedIn Learning (formerly Lynda), YouTube, and Khan Academy.

Why Technical Experience Matters

Many business operations or strategy roles list SQL or other coding knowledge (Python, R, etc.) as a preferred qualification. Although I have no doubt that you can learn this on the job, it's a skill that can help you stand out from the competition and give you a leg up during the interview process. Some interviews for business operations roles will even have a SQL whiteboard interview during the on-site element.

Getting technical experience doesn't necessarily mean getting a master's degree in computer science, data science, or analytics. Although that could be helpful for some, it requires a lot of money and time, and I'd recommend starting off with some online classes and creating a side project where you can apply the skills you learned in class.

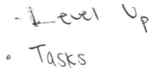

6 Patricia Veng, "Insid
UTS Career Blog, accessed
inside-the-insidesherpa-
7 Zack Friedman, "Her
Forbes, May 29, 2020, htt
free-online-education/#1

I ended up picking up a bit of Python and R during my roles so that I could learn how to automate some of the more repetitive tasks and focus my time and effort on the priorities. These experiences came in handy for the behavioral interview process since I was able to showcase that I'm a proactive learner and problem-solver.

If you don't have a technical background (or your technical skills don't come out on your resume), try to find a way to develop and demonstrate these skills in another way.

The Value of Side Projects

When I was nearing the end of my consulting gig, my dream companies included tech giants like Google and Facebook (now Meta). I tried applying online several times but never heard back.

Since my cold applications weren't gaining traction, I created projects that showcased my research and interests. I then created a website (asun10.github.io) to showcase all these projects. Soon, tech recruiters were visiting my website and reaching out to me instead of the other way around.

The reason I share this story is because it taught me that you should always think outside the box. If you don't have a job or internship for the summer, or if you don't have the experience needed for your dream job, work on your own project to gain that knowledge. Create your own internship. Tailor it toward a company or industry you want to work for. Then, when you're networking, you can tell them you developed a project that supports what they're doing as a business.

By doing this, you'll create a valuable prop for yourself. Instead of doubting yourself and wondering, "What happens if they don't like this?" think of the possibilities that may come from it.

You have nothing to lose but everything to gain.

I'd like to share an example side project that I showcased on my website and expand on my motivation behind it:

When I was in Chicago, I started volunteering at Erie Neighborhood House, a program that provides tutoring primarily for low-income communities. My student wasn't motivated to do homework, and we struggled to even get through each problem set. I decided to write to a local college, the University of Chicago, asking for a donation of anything college-related to help the student stay focused. Right away, they sent her a T-shirt, which both excited her and motivated her to keep learning.

After the success with the university, I decided to get other colleges on board with donations for underprivileged kids. All of a sudden, an idea was formed. I didn't have a lot of time to contact a long list of colleges, so I decided to write a code in Google Apps Script that would enable me to automate my email. This way, I could send requests to sixteen hundred colleges across the nation, including Swarthmore College, Regent College, and the University of California, Irvine. Although I had limited coding experience, I looked up example codes online, pieced them together, tested, and iterated. Finally, I got it to work. Like an avalanche, I began receiving dozens of packages a day containing T-shirts, pamphlets, pens, notebooks, and even toothbrushes, totaling up to more than three thousand items—enough to hugely expand my number of beneficiaries.

With the help of Erie Neighborhood House, we got in contact with a classroom of highly motivated local students. During one afternoon, I donated all the items I had collected to them. Watching their reaction to the gifts was wonderful, as was seeing them eagerly discussing the college pamphlets as they learned more about potential opportunities for higher education. The buzz spread. Later that week, the assistant director of Erie's foundation, Maria Munoz, wrote to me: "Thank you so much for coming and donating, Amy! Kids have been wearing the college shirts all this week."

Looking to light a spark in a student lit a spark in me. In the process, I was able to put my professional skills to use and multiply the results of my efforts. As I learned, a small incentive can go a long way in motivating a student to do the work that will pave their way to college and beyond. There is nothing more rewarding to me than the satisfaction that comes from knowing I made an impact on others' lives in order to help them in a lasting and meaningful way.

This side project gave me the confidence to learn to code and actually inspired me to take on new challenges at work. For example, when I started my new role at Groupon as a BizOps analyst, I was given the task of creating weekly business reports (WBRs). This would essentially be a 50–100-page slide deck on the latest revenue and user trends, split by different regions, industry verticals, and devices (Android versus iPhone). It was incredibly useful for leadership to see how we were performing as a company on a weekly basis, but it was also incredibly boring to populate these charts using an existing dashboard.

I would spend thirty minutes every Monday manually filtering a dashboard by different regions (e.g., China, USA, UK) or verticals (e.g., beauty and wellness, health, travel) and taking screenshots of the charts to place in the deck. After a while, I got tired of this and decided to take it upon myself to automate the process in Python. Luckily, my manager was on board, and I slowly learned through a process of trial and error. I looked up similar scripts online, took pieces of other people's code, pieced it together, and then worked on debugging each error. It took a month to finish the Python script, but it finally worked.

When you pressed the "run" button, the script would refresh the latest dashboard link, scroll the right number of pixels to the appropriate chart, and toggle the filters one by one. Then, it would screenshot each one of the charts and save them as PNG files. Finally, through a Google Slides API, the images were added into Google Slides, and I would automatically have a skeleton deck to work with. This whole process would take less than five minutes. I could grab a coffee and watch Python do the work for me.

4

Understanding the Hiring Process: Behind the Scenes

YOU KNOW THE DRILL. You submit an application online for your dream job, and you check your email every day for a response. Then you wait . . . wait . . . and wait some more. Maybe you'll get an automated letter thanking you for your interest and letting you know they've chosen to move forward with a different candidate. Sometimes there's no follow-up response at all.

Because you have no visibility into the process, you may be wondering, what is actually happening behind the scenes?

In this chapter I'll walk you through how the interview process works at Google, Facebook, and Groupon from my firsthand experience.

What's unique about Google is that even if the team that interviews you likes you, there's still a chance you won't receive an offer. That's because there's also a hiring committee (HC) that gets a say in the decision.

"You will typically have 3 rounds of interviews (one phone screen, one video interview, and one onsite loop) where you meet 5–6 Googlers," writes Niya Dragova for Candor.[8] An on-site inter-

8 Niya Dragova, "Google's Hiring Committee—All the Juicy Details," Candor, May 5, 2020, https://candor.co/interview-prep/google-s-hiring-committee-all-the-deets.

view loop refers to the series of interviews and conversations in your final round with different people in the company. Most of the time, the interview loops are standardized (meaning candidates for a role are put through the same loop of people and questions) to help the interviewers calibrate expectations.

Below, I've broken their internal hiring process down so you can see how each stage fits into the overall timeline.

1. Screening process:
    a. Headcount approval (setting the budget for new hires)
    b. Job requisition and posting
    c. Sourcing candidates
    d. Recruiter phone screen interview
    e. Hiring manager video interview (this may or may not happen, depending on the team)

2. Interview process:
    a. On-site interview (three–four interviews for forty-five minutes each, including with the hiring manager, peers, and typically one cross-functional stakeholder such as a program manager)
    b. Evaluation of the candidate's attributes against Google's values and culture
    c. Interview panel discussion and decision

3. After the interview:
    a. Submission of decision to hiring committee (HC)
    b. Potential for extra interview

c. VP approval

d. Compensation approval

e. Extend offer letter to candidate

As mentioned in chapter 2, interviewers at Google evaluate candidates in one of four different focus areas: role-related knowledge (RRK), general cognitive ability (GCA), leadership, and Googleyness. The RRK part of the rubric looks different from team to team, of course, but the rest remains constant across roles. Let's look at an example of what the requirements are for these four focus areas.

Examples of Role-Related Knowledge (RRK)

- Data Processing: Data extraction and coding (SQL, Python, R), data structure fundamentals
- Statistical Analysis: Experimental design and analysis (randomized and non-randomized), forecasting
- Business Acumen: Structured problem-solving, core metrics derivation, finding creative data-driven solutions and insights for product questions
- Communication: Effective and concise business writing (docs and decks), presenting to management, simple conveyance of complex ideas, visualization tools, focus on impact of analysis

General Cognitive Ability (GCA)

- Communicates clearly
- Understands the problem
- Identifies solutions and supports them with examples

Leadership

- Manages projects
- Ensures that workstreams get completed
- Works well with a team

Googleyness

- Thrives in ambiguity
- Puts the user first
- Does the right thing

If you look online, you might see people talking about very unconventional interview questions that have been asked at Google, such as "Why is a manhole cover round?" or "You're shrunk down to six inches and tossed in a blender. What do you do?" You can disregard them. While I won't say that no brainteaser question like that has ever been asked in a Google interview, they are not the sort of questions you'll get asked today. Instead, expect a mixture of behavioral, technical, and case questions, which we'll explore in more detail in chapters 9 through 11.

Facebook (now Meta)

At Facebook, the hiring process is similar but not as complex:

1. Screening process:
    a. Headcount approval
    b. Job requisition and posting
    c. Sourcing candidates
    d. Recruiter phone screen interview
    e. Hiring manager phone screen interview

2. Interview process:
   a. On-site interview (three–four interviews of forty-five minutes each, including with the hiring manager, peers, and typically one cross-functional stakeholder, such as a product manager)
   b. Evaluation of the candidate's attributes against Facebook's values and culture
   c. Interview panel discussion and decision
   d. Potential for extra interview
   e. Compensation approval
   f. Extend offer letter to candidate

You'll notice that there's always the potential for an extra interview even *after* the on-site rounds. What does this mean? In my experience, this means that you got good feedback but there was a red flag that the team wants clarity on. I've had an additional interview at Facebook after the on-site element, which ended up being with the director (one level above the hiring manager). I suspect that happened because I mentioned that my weakness was that I'd done a lot of operational work and less big-picture strategy work. The director ended up focusing on a strategy case to make sure I had the raw skill set to figure it out.

In my experience, Facebook's hiring process (which takes about one month) has been speedier than Google's (closer to two months), in part because there is no hiring committee to confirm the results.

Groupon

Groupon was the first tech company I worked for. The hiring process was similar to Facebook's and Google's, but it had a few nuances that are worth flagging:

1. Screening process:
    a. Headcount approval
    b. Job requisition and posting
    c. Sourcing candidates
    d. Recruiter phone screen interview
    e. Small case interview through Google Docs
    f. Hiring manager phone screen interview

2. Interview process:
    a. On-site interview
    b. Interview panel discussion and decision

3. After the interview:
    a. VP approval
    b. Compensation approval
    c. Extend offer letter to candidate

Similar to Facebook's, Groupon's hiring process was very quick. There was a one-month turnaround time between my application and when I got my offer letter.

During the screening process, the small case interview via Google Docs asked the following: "You notice that iPhone revenue is declining sharply in Q4'19 compared to previous quarters. What analyses would you want to conduct to understand this trend?"

During the on-site interview process, I had four interviewers in total. This included two managers on the BizOps team, one product manager on the Desktop Discovery team, and one general interviewer called a bar-raiser. A bar-raiser is an interviewer who is brought into the hiring process to be an objective third party. By bringing in someone not associated with the team, they can give an unbiased perspective on the candidates' qualities. They may have higher standards because they aren't worried about filling the job quickly (since they don't work in that department).

Right before my on-site interview, the hiring manager sent an email (included below) that helped me prepare. If either the recruiter or hiring manager gives you hints on what to think about before your big day, make sure to follow their direction and prepare well.

> Hey Amy,
>
> First off, congrats on making it to the final round!
>
> In terms of getting ready for the final round, you'll be interviewing with two managers on the team—a PM we work alongside on the Desktop/Touch Discovery side (redesigning the homepage is an example of something he works on) as well as a general interviewer.
>
> I'd recommend that you really spend time with our app and site if you haven't already. Put yourself in the place of our customer, and then think through what could potentially be improved. We have basically two sets of customers—users who search and users who browse—which makes it difficult to create a single experience that satisfies both use cases. What might be important to one group but not the other?
>
> Don't be afraid to think big picture too—we do a mixture of short-term optimizations and long-term, big strategic bets. If you could totally blow up the experience and start over, what might that feel like?
>
> Our app experience is basically a combination of the ef-

forts of our product team, our marketing team, and our supply team. Deal supply, in particular, is a big question on our minds. We've got a decent amount of merchants in places like Chicago but very little in smaller metropolitan areas. Think through all the challenges and opportunities on the supply side and how you get the product in a spot to make it all work.

There aren't really right or wrong answers here—the real benefit is just putting in the thought. :)

Also take a look at some of our latest earnings detail to get a good feel for what we're focused on as a company.

Finally, think about "Why Groupon?" instead of another tech company—a lot of the perks we have around autonomy, pace, and culture can be found elsewhere. What in particular about Groupon sets itself apart from other tech in your mind?

As always, feel free to let me know if you have any questions.

Take care,

[Hiring manager's name]

After I read the hiring manager's email, I prepared for these specific scenarios. I downloaded the app on both iPhone and Android devices, and I tested the entire sign-up flow, pretending that I was a new user. I noticed the major pain-points from the consumer's perspective and thought about how my actions would be different if I was primarily a searcher versus a browser. I also dug deep into the earnings materials to make sure I knew the big bets that Groupon was focused on in the next year. Last, I prepared my answer for the "Why Groupon?" question and nailed it during the on-site interview.

5

Applying for Jobs: The Power of Referrals

COMPLETING COLD APPLICATIONS ONLINE is a waste of time. Since it's easy to apply for jobs online, you may be competing with hundreds or thousands of other applicants. If you have exactly the right qualifications and experience and a perfectly tailored resume, you might be in the top 25 percent . . . but that's still a long shot.

"The average job has 250 applicants. Only 4 to 6 people will get an interview, and only 1 will be offered the role," according to resume service ZipJob.[9] This is why it's so hard to get a job! Fortunately, you don't need to rely on cold applications to find the position you want. Instead, focus the majority of your time on networking and getting a referral. This can be one of the most productive and fastest ways to ensure you get your dream job.

In this chapter, I'll explore how to begin networking; the power of referrals and how to get them; the etiquette around virtual networking, including what works and what doesn't; and finally, the importance of documenting your applications so that you can keep on top of the process of job hunting.

9 ZipJob team, "5 Reasons Why Applying for Jobs Online Doesn't Work," ZipJob, August 6, 2020, https://www.zipjob.com/blog/applying-for-jobs-online-waste-of-time/.

How to Start Networking

Networking is an investment. It's kind of like building the foundation of a house, but instead, you're building the relationships that will be the foundation of your career. Networking allows you access to opportunities you might not be able to find on your own. Your network has the potential to provide you with insight into different fields, information on what potential employers are looking for, and advice on how you can improve professionally. If you're willing to form and maintain the relationship, a single contact could get you into meetings or interviews with several companies without you having to work to form connections at each one. You might not see immediate returns from networking, but it is never a wasted effort.

Decide on the best networking method for you. Big events are not my thing. As an introvert, I tend to get overwhelmed by big events, and they can be draining for me. Personally, I enjoy one-on-one conversations a lot more, so I prefer to invite people to coffee instead of going to larger, planned events. I find these conversations more useful because I can learn more about the other person, create a real connection, and discuss things in more depth. You can also choose between networking in-person or online, which I'll explore in more detail in this chapter. The benefit of networking online is that you have a wider pool of people to contact, and you're not just limited by your location. The major drawback is that it's harder to read body language and it's easier to misinterpret things. In my opinion, face-to-face conversations are better in the early, formative stages of a relationship when you're just getting to know each other.

If you're nervous in networking situations, prepare a list of stock questions to use when your mind goes blank. "What do you do?" and "Tell me about yourself" are great ways to open up a conversation. It's also helpful to prepare an elevator pitch of what you do as well so you're not put on the spot. There's nothing worse than not being able to succinctly explain your role and how valuable you are when someone asks you this question. This is your opportunity to demonstrate why you're a great contact for them to have.

Sometimes it doesn't even take extra time out of your day to network if you're sitting next to someone on a flight, at a conference, or at a friend's barbecue. When you see someone new or someone you'd like to get to know, just start a conversation and introduce yourself!

Why a Referral Is a Must

A referral from someone in the company you are applying to wins against a cold online application every time. But why?

Put yourself in a recruiter's shoes. If you needed to hire two business operations analysts, would you look at the pile of more than a thousand cold applications or the fifty referrals you have from contacts in the company? Obviously, it would be the fifty referrals. It's a much more manageable task and you trust the people who have passed on these recommendations. They've already provided you with an initial screening process.

This is the answer to your problem. You're not getting rejected because you're not qualified. Rather, you're getting rejected because your resume never gets looked at in the first place. The recruiter finds their qualified candidates in the referral pile. Lesson learned: don't apply, get referred!

Last, not all referrals are equal. If you're able to find the few dozen employees who work for the business unit and product you're applying for, those will offer the most valuable referrals.

How to Get a Referral

A common question I get asked is "How do I get a referral for a company?" The answer is simple: you just ask for one!

Now that we know how important a referral is, let's take a look at how to find the right person for the referral.

Asking Someone You Know Well

The easiest way to get a referral is to ask someone you're already well acquainted with (e.g., a previous coworker, classmate from school, or family friend). You probably already have mutual interests and can make easy conversations. Be straightforward—let them know you're looking for a job and ask them if they'd be willing to help out.

It may feel taboo, but you have to put yourself out there if you need help.

Keep in mind, though, that even if you're asking a close friend for a referral, it's not a guarantee that you'll get one. If someone isn't able to vouch for your work quality or hasn't worked with people in your field before, they might not be comfortable submitting a referral and putting themselves on the line. Because of this, it's polite to give them an exit option rather than jeopardizing the relationship. Here's an example of something you could say to your friend:

> Hi Sarah! Last time we chatted, you mentioned that you really enjoy working at Google! I wonder if I can ask you for a favor, and it's not an issue if you can't help. I'm trying to get my foot in the door at Google, and I think a referral would be really helpful. Would you be able to put in a referral for me for the strategy and operations analyst role? It would really mean a lot. I can attach my resume and walk you through my qualifications if that would be helpful!

If they do end up referring you, don't take it for granted. Take them out to dinner or get them a small thank-you present for their help.

Asking Someone You Don't Know Well

You know that classmate from Calculus I whom you only spoke to a handful of times? Or that friend of a friend you met at a barbecue? Well, even those connections can come in handy. When you reach out to someone you don't know well, make it a point to remind them of any commonalities you two may share. By providing context about your relationship, you can establish your credibility.

> Hi Emma, it was so great meeting you through our mutual friend Christine last week at her barbecue! I remember you mentioned that you're at Meta now and have been enjoying your new role. I've started to think about transitioning jobs, and I saw an open role on the BizOps team at Meta and wanted to reach out. Do you mind if I impose on you? I'd love to hear more about your experience so far at Meta. I also think it could be helpful to tell you more about my background so that you know a bit more about me!

The last part is key because people we only know peripherally on a social basis might have little knowledge about our background. It's good to share any relevant information that they might be unaware of and that might even impress them. That way, if they do put in a referral for you, they'll leave comments for the hiring managers and recruiters, which will help them to get a better sense of what you have to offer.

Just as you would with a friend, it's a nice gesture to express your appreciation for the referral with a thank-you note or small gift.

Asking Someone You Don't Know

You may not have a connection at every company you apply to, and that's okay. There are kind strangers out there who are willing to help—you just need to put in the effort to look for them online and reach out. Keep your eye out for recruiters, managers who have "I'm hiring" in their headline, and employees who have the role title you're interested in. When you cold message someone you don't know, try to bring up anything that you may have in common. For example, if you both went to University of Michigan, you can introduce yourself by saying that you're also a Michigan alumna.

Start by expressing your interest in the role and trying to get to know this person. Instead of asking for help too quickly, restructure your request so that it's a conversation rather than a transaction.

> Hi Chris, I know we recently connected on LinkedIn as University of Michigan alumni. I noticed that the BizOps team at your company has an open position, and I'm interested. Any chance I could ask you a few questions about the company and role?

If they accept and schedule a call, great! Use your interest as a way to start the conversation, and then be open to where it leads. First, start off with asking questions about company culture, the day-to-day responsibilities of the role, and what they love about working there. Then, you can gently segue into mentioning you want to work at the company. Have a strong pitch ready for why you want this referral, what you can bring to the table, how this can help you accomplish your goals, and why you believe they can help you. All this context is necessary because you're essentially asking a stranger to open doors for you.

Last, it's important that you thank them for their time and keep them posted on your application status. This way, they feel more involved and will likely be more willing to help you in the future.

If you don't get the referral the first time, don't worry! Say something like this: "Thanks again for your time! Who else would you suggest I connect with on the team to learn more about the role?" By doing this, you can speak with another person and repeat the same cycle, which, again, may lead to a referral. Although it can be challenging and uncomfortable to ask a stranger a favor, it is an incredibly useful skill. Be polite, be grateful, and make it very easy for each person to refer you and help you in your career. Eventually, you can give back and pay the favor forward to others.

The last thing to keep in mind is that many companies have a referral bonus program, so employees are actually incentivized to refer qualified people for full-time roles. So, you don't need to feel bad asking for a referral because it could end up being a win-win situation: you win the job and the referrer wins a nice cash bonus!

The Dos and Don'ts of Virtual Networking

Online networking is the most popular form of making professional connections for obvious reasons. It allows you to easily move beyond your local network, and there are several sites that make it simple to expand and track your network throughout your career. However, there are some common mistakes that people make that are important to avoid, considering online networking is often the way that potential employers (and those who may give you a referral) will first meet you. Here are some basic but very effective strategies that I've employed while networking online that make it easy to give a good first impression and avoid turning people off.

Do

Do fill out professional networking profiles completely. Professional sites like LinkedIn can connect you with potential employers, and their first impression of you will be from your profile. It only takes twenty to thirty minutes of quality time to complete your profile, and it could be the difference between getting the job or not. Some easy fixes include updating your experience section, using a clear and professional photo, and asking for personal recommendations.

Do be your authentic self. While this may sound simple, there are a lot of people who get caught up in trying to be the best candidate and end up force-fitting themselves into a certain position. However, in reality, it's better for the company to understand who you really are.

Do run a spell check. Enough said.

Don't

Don't mix business and pleasure. Make sure you keep your social media accounts separate from your business ones. This way, potential employers will be less likely to see you engage in behavior they might consider unprofessional.

Don't be a nuisance. If someone has already denied your friend request or connection request, don't continue to add them over and over again. Similarly, if someone doesn't respond to your messages after your second approach, continuing to ask will be annoying and only make you seem desperate. Just like advice for dating—there are plenty of fish in the sea! No need to get stuck on just one.

Documenting Your Application Process

Between searching for jobs, sending in applications, taking phone screen interviews, and getting in-person interviews, there's a lot to keep track of while job hunting. With the sheer number of applications you're likely getting through, it's easy to lose track of things along the way.

I like to use a simple spreadsheet to document my application process and keep everything in one place for quick and easy access. That way, when a recruiter reaches back out to me, I know exactly which job title I applied for and what information I gave on the application, and I can reference the right terminology from the job posting if needed. Including other pieces of information in your spreadsheet, such as the job description link, is helpful to ensure you don't waste time going back and searching for the information you need. Including the date you applied also helps you keep track of when you should follow up and when to assume it's a no if you haven't heard back.

Here's a list of the general information I include in my spreadsheet:

- Company name
- Position applied for
- Job posting/description link
- Date applied
- Status of application (e.g., yes, no, never heard back)
- Current stage of hiring process (e.g., applied, phone screen, on-site interview)
- Version of resume used
- Have I sent a follow-up email? Y/N
- Have I sent thank-you emails to interviewers? Y/N

There's not a right or wrong way to use the spreadsheet. You can customize it so that it works best for you. For example, if you enjoy color coding, you can use conditional formatting to make your data easier to interpret at a glance. Green means you have an offer, yellow means you will be interviewing, and red means you've been rejected.

A bullet journal is another great option if you prefer to use pen and paper instead.

6

Writing a Successful BizOps Resume

YOUR EXPERIENCE WON'T LAND you an interview on its own; it's how your resume portrays that experience that matters. Even the best candidates wouldn't get an interview with a poor resume. That's why it's important for you to express your skills and accomplishments in a clear, concise, and effective way.

In this chapter, I'll explain what makes a great BizOps resume, including detailed explanations of what to include and exclude and how to personalize it for the specific role you're applying for. At the end, I've included three successful resumes that should give you a clear idea of what works well and how to articulate and present your own experience.

Making It through the Screening Process

One thing people may not know is that a resume is often not read; at best, it's skimmed.

Since a recruiter receives so many resumes, it's not feasible to carefully go through each one. It's likely that an automated system such as an applicant tracking system (ATS) will screen your resume first. ATS is a human resources software that recruiters and hiring managers use to collect and sort resumes. As of 2021, "Ninety-nine percent of Fortune 500 companies use an ATS as part of their recruiting strategy."[10] Because ATS is automated, it's important that when you write your resume, you mirror exactly the keywords in the job description and requirements listed. This is how ATS will confirm that you are qualified for the job.

Once the automated system deems you qualified, a resume screener will glance through your resume for about fifteen seconds to make a decision about whether or not to interview you. Therefore, once you have all the keywords in your resume, you should then be optimizing the document specifically for this fifteen-second skim.

Attributes of a Good BizOps Resume: Tips and Tricks

Writing a good resume is crucial if you want to clearly demonstrate your education, work experience, and skills. It should communicate how your qualifications fit into the role you're applying for. Employers select applicants if their resume is tailored to the job application, as this shows that you can perform the duties outlined.

Now that you understand why writing a good resume is important, we'll cover the characteristics of what makes a good BizOps resume.

Shorter Is Better

Imagine that I wanted to tell you as much about myself as I could, but your attention span is only fifteen seconds. Should I give you a 500-page autobiography or a condensed, one-paragraph summary?

While the 500-page version will have much more information, that doesn't matter. In fifteen seconds, you'd only make it through the first paragraph and barely learn where I was born. Even though

10 "Applicant Tracking Systems: A Guide for Job Seekers," Job Scan, January 18, 2021, https://www.jobscan.co/applicant-tracking-systems.

I offered more information, you actually learned a lot less about me.

A long resume is similar. It takes all your best content and mixes it with less important information, which leaves the reader with a worse overall impression of you. It's best just to stick to the highlights. A good rule of thumb is to limit your resume to one page if you've had less than ten years of experience.

At what point should I remove internship experience from my resume?

As a general rule, for most people, that time will be somewhere between five and ten years after graduation. It should come off when you feel it no longer strengthens your candidacy or presents a picture of who you are. Since I did internships in engineering and medicine during college, I leave those off my resume since they're not relevant to the jobs I'm applying for. No need to waste valuable space!

Now, there are definitely exceptions where it makes sense to keep your internships on your resume for more than a few years. For example, if you have any impressive or unusual experiences, feel free to keep them. Something prestigious like interning at NASA or the White House can help you stand out from the crowd. A recruiter might want to reach out just to hear that story and see how you and your career have evolved since then. To make this a bit more intuitive, put yourself in the employer's shoes: Would you rather hire a candidate who has only had one job or someone who has had one job *and* spent their time in college getting work experience?

At age forty, what you did in college probably isn't going to matter as much. However, when college was only a few years ago, it's still relevant.

Use Bullet Points Rather Than Blobs of Text

Not only should the resume be short, but the text should be split into bullet points that make it easy to consume (see my earlier point about the fifteen-second skim!). If you see any blobs of text that are more than three lines in your resume, cut them down.

Show Impact, Don't List Responsibilities

Responsibilities are things you're told to do, but they don't often clearly state if you actually had an impact. Instead, focus on accomplishments, and prove to the resume screener that you did in fact have a tangible impact.

Look at the difference between these two statements:

> **Responsibility oriented:** Responsible for forecasting revenue for Google Cloud and helping with headcount planning.
>
> **Accomplishment oriented:** Proactively identified and prioritized revenue levers and opportunities for Google to drive an additional $10 million in revenue.

Stick with a Simple Template

You want to stand out, but your resume template is not the way to go about it. There are lots of resume designs published online that are flashy, use infographic-style charts, or mimic the layout of an iOS phone screen. While these resumes are cute and creative, they're generally going to get the wrong kind of attention (unless you're applying for a designer position).

Many hiring managers I've spoken with hate these graphical resumes because they're hard to read. The information isn't presented in a clear way, and design elements take up more space than necessary.

A good resume template won't necessarily make people exclaim "ooh" and "ahh," but it will convey the information in a clear and accessible way, which will ultimately land you the interview.

Look for a resume template with the following:

Easy-to-read company names and job titles: This information should be easy to pick out, especially if you have a name-brand company on your resume. Location and dates are less important. While they should still be there, they don't need to stand out to the resume screener.

Effective use of space: Avoid left-hand columns that are just for headings. Some resume templates use the left side of the page to highlight fancy headings for "Employment" and "Education" sections. While this looks nice, it can waste up to 20 percent of the available space.

Simple text styles: Having many fonts or colors can be distracting and make it harder to consume the information.

Sufficient white space: White space can be tricky: too much wastes space, but too little can make your resume difficult to read.

Bullets: Big blocks of text can look nice, but they'll generally be skimmed or skipped over, so it's better to stick to bullets.

Include What's Interesting, Even If It's Unfinished

This may seem obvious; however, many candidates leave something valuable out because it wasn't completed or is in process. For example, "We haven't finished publishing yet" or "We didn't get many downloads in the app store." Think to yourself if there's anything you forgot to include that falls into this category and clearly demonstrates your skills or strengths. Are there any projects you've done for school or a friend's company that you haven't listed? Perhaps you've been involved in a hackathon or another activity that demonstrates relevant work skills. If you think it will help you become a more interesting and attractive candidate, go ahead and list it.

What to Include and What to Cut

Your resume will certainly include your work experience and education, but what about the other details? There's only so much space on the page, and as I said previously, you'll want to keep it as concise and focused as possible. It's worth being brutal about what information will help you get to interview and what is just "nice to know." Let's look at the common components of a resume and whether they are truly essential or not.

Objective Statement: No

Most objective statements are just there to take up space: for example, "Experienced analytics leader with a bias for action, seeking a strategy role in a fast-paced, growing environment."

Show, don't tell! There's no need to say "experienced" since that is something that should be clearly shown in the resume. The "bias for action" comment is subjective and anyone can make that claim. The description of the company is also unhelpful since you've applied and are interested regardless of whether it's fast-paced or not.

Objective statements are a verbose description of the role you're applying for, and there's no need to restate what will already be clear on your resume.

Summary: No

I've seen a few rare exceptions, but in my opinion, a summary is rarely useful. If your resume is concise, it already *is* a summary. There's no need to resummarize it in paragraph form.

Skills: Yes

For many positions, especially if there are technical skill requirements, it's useful to include a skills section on your resume because this tells the recruiter whether you can do the job or if you'll need further training. Some examples of skills include SQL, Excel, and Salesforce.

List language skills (e.g., "fluent in Spanish") only if they're relevant to the job you want. Know that your resume space is valuable real estate and every part of it should help you sell yourself to the future employer.

Awards: Yes

You should list awards you've received, even if they're not directly related to the job, since they're often relevant in demonstrating your hard work, success, or creativity. The only caveat here is that you should make your awards mean something to the reader. Oftentimes, candidates will list awards like this:

- Charles R. Westgate Scholarship in Engineering

A resume screener will have no idea what this means. What's this awarded for? How selective is it? You can't expect them to do the research themselves. Thus, your resume should describe what the award is for and how selective it is. For example, you could list it as follows:

- Awarded the Charles R. Westgate Scholarship, a full-tuition scholarship from Johns Hopkins University, awarded to two students each year who demonstrate leadership, academic excellence, and success in independent research

Activities: Maybe

Depending on the activity and how far you've taken it, this section may be useful. The more relevant the activity is to the job, the better it is to list it. For example, activities that use financial modeling or technical skills can be seen as applicable for a BizOps role.

If the activity itself isn't relevant, it could still be good to list it if you've achieved something notable. For example, listing running isn't relevant for most roles (unless it's a fitness company), but if you completed five half-marathons worldwide and have a lifetime goal of hitting fifteen, then it could show ambition, determination, and grit.

If you can back each of your activities up with a concrete accomplishment in this way, then go for it. Otherwise, if you're one of the many people listing hiking as an activity, this section won't mean much to the screener.

Projects: Yes

This section is about projects you undertake in your spare time rather than at work, and I'd recommend that you add this section right after your work experience. I view this section as incredibly important because a side project can provide you with relevant and valuable experience and the opportunity to work on a skill you wouldn't otherwise be able to in your job. If you're a recent graduate, you can include class projects here. You'll want to describe what your project was and how successful it was. For example:

- Automated T-shirts project: Wrote a script to send emails to 5,000+ universities' admissions offices to ask for T-shirts. Received over 100 shirts and donated all the items to local high schoolers (first-generation college students) to inspire them to go to college.

This description clearly shows your responsibilities in the project and quantifies your impact.

Personal Website: Yes

If you have a regularly updated website or blog, include the URL on your resume. If you don't have a website, consider building one. GitHub hosts free websites and you can sign up for an account at github.com. I just followed online tutorials that taught me how to pick a template and make modifications, and the process was relatively straightforward. Some other great options for free website builders include Wix, WordPress, and Weebly.

Your website should provide your resume as well as more details about your projects. It's a good idea to include screenshots for articles you've written, press you've gotten, lectures you've given, and so on. Try to keep the website professional since it's likely that your interviewers will check this out.

Social Media Accounts: Maybe

If you're active on social media about technology or something work-related, this could be valuable to add. Just make sure not to mix business with personal, and remember to remove any old posts that may be controversial or reflect poorly on you.

College Details: Depends

The more years you're out of college, the fewer details you should include on your resume. You can use the following guidance for deciding when to exclude items:

Club member: Just participating in a club doesn't say anything special about you. If you didn't hold a leadership position, this can be removed from your resume once you've graduated (if not sooner).

Leadership positions: If you were the president of a club or had a major accomplishment as a leader, you could justify keeping these on your resume three to five years after graduation.

Founding accomplishments: Founding a sport, club, nonprofit, or other major activity shows you have initiative and the ability to get things done. Therefore, you can justify having this on your resume for five to eight years, depending on how significant the accomplishment was.

Awards: An impressive award like Forbes 30 under 30 should go on your resume and can stay for ten years or longer. By contrast, less impressive awards, like winning third place at a case competition in college, should probably be removed within two years of graduating.

GPA: Depends

If you're just a few years out of school, you can list your GPA if it's above a 3.0 out of 4.0. If you're more than five years out of school, you'll only want to list it if it's 3.5 or above. Basically, you only want to include something historical if it still makes you stand out. If your GPA is exceptional (for example, 4.0), you could keep it indefinitely since it doesn't take up much space on your resume.

If your school doesn't calculate GPA on a 4.0 system, try to translate it for the resume scanner since it can be hard for others to understand what your GPA means. For example, you could add on "(equivalent to 3.4/4.0)" or list it in terms of class rank or percentile.

Some schools have a QPA, which is determined by the courses

required by your major. If this value is higher than your GPA, it may be worth including.

Online Courses: Depends

Showing that you have a passion for learning is great, and you should try to list well-recognized online courses on your resume. However, there are a lot of free online courses out there, and some are not as legitimate as others. Some examples of online organizations that I consider legitimate are General Assembly, Stanford Continuing Studies, and MIT OpenCourseWare. Keep in mind that some of these are free, but others require payment since they are live classes with instructors. Don't forget to check if you get tuition assistance from your current employer as part of your compensation package. You may be able to get these course tuition costs reimbursed through your current employer.

I tend to prioritize listing courses in which I've received a grade. For example, I've listed Stanford Continuing Education courses in which I received a grade and credit. Just try to use your discretion with this. My rule of thumb is the easier it was to receive a "certificate" (e.g., no homework involved), the more likely you should exclude it from your resume.

Ultimately, though, it doesn't matter how many courses you've taken. The goal is to show how you've used this knowledge. Be prepared to talk about a project in which you've applied the knowledge from a course.

Personalizing for the Job Description

Most people make the mistake of submitting the same resume for every job. As mentioned at the beginning of this chapter, many employers use software called an applicant tracking system, known as ATS. An ATS software is supposed to weed out applicants' resumes based on keywords in the job description. If you want to pass this initial electronic screen, your professional resume needs to be tailored for a specific position so it'll indicate to the ATS robots that you're a good fit. That will help you get your application one step closer to the hiring manager's inbox.

Before you submit your resume for a job, put it side by side with the application online and double-check that it includes all the minimum qualifications on it. It sounds simple, but these things can easily be missed and can make all the difference!

The following are four steps you should take to personalize your resume:

1. *Read the job description carefully for keywords.*

Carefully read the job posting, and pay attention to the job title, duties and responsibilities, requirements, and location of the position. Do you notice any keywords and phrases that are repeated throughout the job description? If so, make a list of these key terms and utilize them in your resume where appropriate. For example, highlight the skills and responsibilities you've had in previous roles that echo the keywords they use.

2. *Match your previous job titles to the target job title.*

One common resume strategy is to modify your previous job title to (1) make it easier for resume readers to understand what you've done and (2) show how it is relevant to the current role at hand. This is perfectly acceptable since job titles can vary so much among companies. BizOps is a prime example of this—BizOps roles can be called business operations analyst or associate, strategy and operations analyst or associate, business analyst, and so on. Thus, feel free to adjust your title and use a common or alternative title that makes more sense and is better understood.

However, while you do have flexibility to change "data scientist" to "data analyst," you can't say you were "vice president." That would be lying. There are limits to how much flexibility you have.

3. Tailor your skills to match the language of the job description.

Not only should you meet all the job requirements in terms of qualifications, you should also incorporate keywords associated with those qualifications to make it past the ATS software. If your description does not align with the terminology used by the employer, this could lead to you being weeded out erroneously.

Let's look at an example of employer requirements alongside a resume.

> **Requirements for consideration:** Advanced knowledge of Microsoft applications (Word, Excel, PowerPoint).
>
> **Current resume:** Solid background in Microsoft Suite.

Currently, your resume is missing important keywords—Office, applications, Word, Excel, PowerPoint—that could keep it from passing the ATS screening process, never to be seen by a human being. Instead, adjust your resume to match the language used in the description:

> **Updated resume:** Advanced knowledge of Microsoft Office applications: Word, Excel, and PowerPoint.

Continue incorporating key terms and phrases from the job description into your resume, as long as they describe skills you actually possess. If you don't have that skill, don't lie and include it. You could be tested on that skill later down the line.

4. Confirm your location if it's local.

Some employers tend to favor local candidates because they're less expensive to hire (think relocation costs, travel expenses during the interview process, etc.) and less likely to get flakey and jump ship because of the strain and inconvenience of moving to a new city.

So, if you're searching for a job nearby, make sure employers know you're a local candidate by including your location in the contact information at the top of your resume.

Otherwise, if you are planning to relocate to a place near the job you are applying for, make sure to let your potential employer know you're open to relocation. They'll usually be more sensitive to your situation and not quickly dismiss your resume because of location issues.

Real Resumes That Landed the Role

I thought it would be valuable to give real-world examples of resumes that were successful in landing BizOps roles in tech. I'll start with my own and then show several anonymized resumes from my colleagues at Google.

Amy Yan

This resume succeeds at mirroring the job description and skills needed for the role I applied for. I used keywords like "SQL," "Python," "forecasts," and "dashboard" to ensure that ATS would not filter my resume out. I also included extracurriculars that help my resume stand out to recruiters.

One of the critiques I have looking back at my resume is that I listed that I was "awarded the Westgate Full Tuition Scholarship to Johns Hopkins University." As mentioned previously in this chapter, a resume screener wouldn't know how selective this is and would likely not have time to do the research themselves. I would recommend either removing this or adding more clarifying detail if there's space left.

This was the resume submitted that helped me land my first role at Google as a strategy and operations analyst.

Amy Yan

PROFESSIONAL EXPERIENCE

Business Operations Analyst

Facebook App, Facebook, Menlo Park, CA
Jan 2019–present

- Build revenue forecasts, analyze current business performance, and assess market opportunities for Facebook.
- Use SQL to analyze revenue and engagement data, develop actionable insights, and present recommendations to product and finance leadership that enable revenue and engagement growth.
- Quantify the value/size of new opportunities to inform and prioritize product roadmaps.
- Identify, develop, and track product and financial metrics by building Tableau dashboards.

Senior Analyst

Business Operations, Groupon, Chicago, IL
Jan 2018–Jan 2019

- Partnered with product teams to identify and drive strategic and operational improvements that deliver sustainable growth.
- Analyzed A/B mobile experiments using SQL queries to measure the impact of new features, understand how users are interacting with the new features, and determine if

there are any further optimizations that could be made to generate more lift.

- Developed data pipelines from raw clickstream logs to track week-over-week business metrics, as well as performance toward achieving product goals.
- Built Tableau dashboard tools to better understand how users are interacting with Groupon's offerings.
- Developed Python code to automate weekly business review meeting decks.

Business Analyst

McKinsey & Company, Atlanta, GA
July 2016–Jan 2018

- Managed the onboarding of banks, timing of deliverables, and stakeholder communications for a benchmark of 26 banks that represent $346 billion in average daily collected balances and $1.9 billion in cumulative annual fee revenues.
- Automated data validation and clients' onboarding process with Python to reduce the error rate by 25%.
- Used SQL to develop new data-driven benchmarking strategies within financial services that cleaned and standardized multi-client data.
- Created Tableau dashboards and stories to measure treasury management portfolio growth against industry benchmark; developed MS Excel pricing model to calculate the most efficient repricing strategy for clients.
- Conducted data scrubbing and detailed analysis of the study participants in "The Federal Reserve Payments Study 2016."

- Interacted with clients to explain the questionnaire of "The Federal Reserve Payments Study" and advise on their mid- to long-term opportunities.

EDUCATION

Johns Hopkins University, Baltimore, MD

Sep 2012–May 2016

- BS in biomedical engineering and BS in engineering mechanics (dual degree).
- President and valedictorian of JHU Class of 2016 (Student Government Association).
- Awarded the Westgate Full Tuition Scholarship to Johns Hopkins University.

SKILLS

SQL, Excel, Tableau, Python, R, Alteryx, MATLAB, PowerPoint

EXTRACURRICULARS

The Little Stars Foundation:

- Founder of 501(c)(3) nonprofit charitable organization in 2007.

- Led a group of young musicians to perform over a hundred free concerts to local nursing homes; visited over a thousand seniors in metro Detroit and fundraised over $7,000 for the organization.

Born This Way Foundation:

- Channel Kindness writer/reporter for Lady Gaga's Born This Way Foundation; wrote and published articles that documented acts of generosity, compassion, and acceptance.
- Published a chapter in Lady Gaga's book, *Channel Kindness.*

Hopkins Sports Taekwondo:

- Fourth-degree black belt instructor (master level); USA Taekwondo Association official referee.

Jane Doe

This resume succeeds at quantifying Jane's impact during her projects: e.g., "oversaw creation and execution of exit-TSA cutover plan for a $10b global beauty integration . . ." Through this word choice, Jane was able to demonstrate tangible impact rather than just stating her responsibilities.

One of the critiques I have looking at this resume is that there are two bullets that are very similar:

- Elected to 130th Business Board, which oversees company's business strategy.
- Served on 130th Executive Board, company's overarching leadership for day-to-day strategy.

I would recommend consolidating to one bullet and making sure to proofread the resume a few more times before submitting.

This was the resume Jane submitted to Google that landed her a Strategy & Operations Manager role.

Jane Doe

EXPERIENCE

Strategy& (formerly Booz & Co., now part of the PwC network)

Associate (Aug 2016–Dec 2018)

- Developed high-level growth strategy for an online and print sports magazine looking to expand their offerings and market reach.
- Analyzed the sports media and analytics markets to understand trends; defined growth opportunities.
- Led customer interviews to understand unmet needs and drivers of willingness to spend.
- Prioritized industry hot spots and assessed how current brands and offerings could be expanded.
- Assessed high-level capabilities and enablers needed for client to pursue the recommended strategy.
- Recommended high-level strategy for financial services client in a data and analytics digital transformation as part of a global restructuring project.
- Oversaw creation and execution of exit-TSA cutover plan for a \$10b global beauty integration to transition the organization's business, systems, and processes while minimizing any impact

to the company's overall business and ensuring order fulfillment before, during, and after system shut-down and go-live.

- Served as client staff lead for Strategy& recruiting at Penn.
- Earned highest rating given to first-year associates at annual performance review.

The New York Times

Retention Marketing Intern (June 2015–Aug 2015)

- Conducted thorough competitive analysis to improve communications with all active, potential, and former subscribers; presented research and recommendations to team and senior staff.
- Developed email campaigns targeting former subscribers in order to engage and reactivate paid subscriptions; tracked, monitored, and reported metrics to shape future campaigns.
- Analyzed and optimized email communication series for Dunning customers to drive incremental revenue.
- Created product along with tech interns to increase engagement and improve reader experience; determined goals, impact, and marketing strategy.

The Daily Pennsylvanian

Advertising Manager (Jan 2014–Dec 2014)

- Hired, trained, and managed student staff of 10; created revenue goals and new advertising opportunities.
- Elected to 130th Business Board, which oversees company's business strategy.

- Served on 130th Executive Board, company's overarching leadership for day-to-day strategy.
- First FY with revenue growth since FY 2008; first semester with operational profit since 2008.

The Daily Pennsylvanian

Advertising Representative, Sept 2012–Dec 2013

- Sold over $30,000 of advertising space in 2013 in daily campus newspaper to businesses as top sales rep.
- January 2013 Business Member of the Month; 2013 Business Staff Member of the Year.

EDUCATION

University of Pennsylvania

BA in economics and BA in music, 2016.

John Doe

This resume succeeds at being concise while also impressive. John uses easy-to-read company names and job titles so that the information is easy to pick out. John holds an MBA from Harvard and also has a PhD with a high GPA. He clearly looks good on paper.

One of the critiques I have looking at this resume is that it doesn't seem like John personalized his resume to fit the job description. I would recommend that he take a closer look at the job posting and make sure to mirror that language to stand out.

This was the resume John submitted to Google that landed him a Strategy & Operations Associate role.

John Doe

PROFESSIONAL EXPERIENCE

Graduate Student Researcher

University of California, Merced
Aug 2009–Dec 2014

- Initiated and carried out independent research projects in the area of biomaterials for applications in drug delivery, biosensing, optics, and photonics using experimental techniques such as SEM, AFM imaging, and FEA computer simulations.
- Authored manuscripts for journal and conference submission, obtaining acceptance of 10 oral presentations at conferences.
- Mentored 30 students in lab sessions of materials science, materials selection and performance, and simulations.
- Developed lab protocols and materials for students in microscopy, X-ray diffraction, polymers, and metallography.

Consultant

Stanford Office of Technology Licensing
Oct 2013–Dec 2013

- Investigated potential applications of an innovative positioning device with haptic features for surgery applications and developed a written report and oral presentation.

Analyst Intern

Morgan Stanley
Jan 2012–Mar 2012

- Created financial reports of engineering-based companies using fundamental analysis of their financial information for making predictions and long-term investment decisions.

Entrepreneur

Opcion Gama
May 2006–June 2008

- Founded and managed a startup to commercialize polymeric adhesives and supplies for the footwear industry in Colombia.
- Developed territory, led aggressive sales plans increasing sales 25%, YOY, and high customer retention.
- Expanded the business into a second branch in Venezuela and carried out import/export operations.

EDUCATION

- MBA, Harvard Business School (spring 2019)
- PhD, University of California, Merced, materials science engineering (spring 2015). GPA 3.92.
- BS, Universidad Industrial de Santander, Colombia, chemical engineering (fall 2005). GPA 3.80.
- Ignite Program, Stanford University (spring 2017)

This program expands on the fundamentals of business and the process of evaluating business ideas and product design.

AWARDS

- UC Merced Graduate Fellowship (2013 and 2014).
- Miguel Velez Fellowship (2011 and 2013).
- UC Merced School of Engineering Fellowship (2012).
- Colfuturo Fellowship (2010).
- UC Merced Graduate Division Scholarship (2010).
- Heinz Foundation Scholarship (2009).

LEADERSHIP

- Member of the National Diversity Committee of the Materials Research Society (2010–2015).
- Society of Hispanic Professional Engineers (SHPE)—Regional Graduate Representative (2010–2012).
- University of California, Merced, Materials Research Society Chapter—Founder President (2010–2011).

OUTREACH ACTIVITIES

- Mentor of undergraduate students at Mentor-room through a sponsored program by Google (Oct 2016–present).
- English as a second language (ESL) teaching assistant for minorities (janitors) at Google (Apr 2015–2017 & 2019–present).
- Society of Hispanic Professional Engineers (SHPE) volunteer, San Jose, CA (Oct 2011–2014).

7

Researching the Company: Your Secret Weapon

When you're preparing for a job interview, gather every bit of information about the company that you can. This will be your secret weapon to help you stand out from your competition. Completing this research not only shows that you take initiative but also reflects your enthusiasm for the company and role. It takes time to collect the necessary information, so I'd recommend you start this process as soon as you have the interview scheduled.

In this chapter, I'll outline some of the best sources of information to support your research. Then we'll look at each component that you need to consider: the employer's mission, their culture, the role you're applying for, and the products you will be working with.

Finding Information Sources

There are innumerable sources of information that you could use to research the company you're applying to. I've listed a few key resources that I've found particularly helpful in my own job searches.

10-K Annual Reports

All public companies are required to file an annual disclosure on financial performance following the close of their fiscal year, and this is called a Form 10-K. This can be found on the company website or the US Securities and Exchange Commission government website under "Filings."[11] The 10-K is a comprehensive document that is a great starting point for learning more about the company. Specifically, it will tell you about

- the company's products and service offerings,
- the company's financial performance,
- major competitors,
- recent events,
- risks to the business, and
- the company's outlook.

If the company is private and doesn't have a 10-K, they may still publish an annual report for their investors that you can look for online.

Tech Articles

Tech articles are another great source of information. These are written by a range of different media companies. My personal favorite news source is TechCrunch, but others include the Verge, *Wired*, Mashable, and Tech Radar. These articles provide news and perspectives on tech companies from an outsider's perspective, while the 10-K is an insider report that comes from the company itself. Thus, the information in tech articles will provide a broader range of view on the company and help you develop opinions that build on the more factual data of the 10-K.

Tech articles will give you useful information on companies:

11 "EDGAR Company Filings," US Securities and Exchange Commission, accessed December 27, 2021, https://www.sec.gov/edgar/searchedgar/companysearch.html.

- Recent events and how these events might impact customers, competition, or the company's future
- Different viewpoints on how the company is performing
- Opinions on what the company should be doing differently

Talking to Employees and Alumni

Try to find and connect with at least one person who is a current or former employee of the company you're interested in interviewing for and set up a time to chat. Ideally, speak with someone who worked in the same role or team you're interviewing for. Start by using your own network, and if you can't find a connection, look to cold message people using the techniques I outlined in chapter 3. You could perhaps meet in person for a coffee if they're local, or otherwise you could video chat.

Setting up an informal chat with employees will give you inside information on the following:

- The culture of the company
- The skills and attributes that the company values
- What the day-to-day role is like (e.g., responsibilities, tasks)
- How this role and team fit within the broader organization
- The work-life balance in the team and the organization more broadly
- Preferable working styles of people on the team

This information is harder to find online as it's based on people's experiences rather than reports or requirements generated by the company itself, so finding a source can be incredibly valuable in giving you a head start over other candidates.

Analyst Reports

Financial analysts (e.g., investment banking analysts) write reports to provide guidance to investors. You can find these kinds of reports through online platforms such as Capital IQ, Morningstar, Thomson Reuters, and Argus Research Company. The only issue is that you'll need a subscription to access these services.

If you can't get a subscription through your current company, you can find less detailed summaries of analyst reports through sites like Robinhood, Yahoo! Finance, NASDAQ, and so on. You'll find three different kinds of analyst reports: initiating coverage reports, company analyst reports, and industry reports.

Initiating coverage reports get released when a brokerage firm is covering a company for the very first time; they cover history, trends, and competitors. These brokerage firms typically employ stock analysts to study companies and issue recommendations that are passed on, such as "hold," "long-term buy," or "market outperform."

Company analyst reports focus on financial performance but have some qualitative analysis.

Industry reports provide a much broader perspective on the industry as a whole, including details on market sizes, market share of key companies, and major trends. Similar to the first two types of reports, industry reports aren't written by the company itself but can still provide in-depth insight into the industry the company is playing in. For example, learning about the digital advertising spend by region can help you understand where the major regional focuses will be for players like Google and Meta, and you can form an opinion about where the company should expand to next.

Professional Community Forums

Blind is an app and website (teamblind.com) that provides an anonymous forum and community for verified employees to discuss issues about their company. Users are grouped by topic, organization, and their broader industry. You can use it to find frank opinions from employees across industries about the workplace environment, salaries, and promotion timelines.

Before interviewing with a company or team, it would be beneficial to see if anyone has posted about the interview process on Blind. You can also see what employees are concerned or gossiping about.

People also post asking the crowd to chime in on advice about which of multiple offers to take (Netflix or Amazon?), whether to jump ship from a current job, where to look for jobs that will sponsor an H-1B visa, and whether or not the comments on Glassdoor represent the company fairly.

Glassdoor is a bit of an older resource. It's a website where current and former employees anonymously review companies and submit salaries. You'll also be able to find new job postings and apply directly to companies through Glassdoor. In my opinion, it's best to check both of these resources for the role and company you're interested in so you can get as much information as possible about the interview process, the day-to-day role, pros and cons of the company, and estimated salary ranges.

Now that we've looked at the various sources of information available, let's consider what key elements you should be researching.

Company Mission

You should know not only what the company is doing but why it's doing it. Understanding the "why" will help you structure your answers to fit the company's vision and view of the world. For example, if the company wants to "bring the world closer together," then talk about why that's important to you.

Knowing the "why" means getting a good grasp of the following:

Mission: Look up the company's mission statement, which should be on the company website in a "Company Info" or "Investor Info" section. How well does it live up to its mission? Think about specifics and examples so you can demonstrate your knowledge and stand out during the interview process. For example, consider the Starbucks mission statement: "To inspire and nurture the human spirit—one person, one cup and one neighborhood at a time."[12] Notice that the mission isn't to sell the most coffee or even make the best-tasting coffee—it's more ambitious than that. Instead, its mission is to develop a human connection with customers through coffee, and that's something its employees can get behind. If I were interviewing at Starbucks, I would make sure to tie my answers back to the focus on creating a great customer experience above all else. Make sure you take advantage of whatever you discover, showing off how well your values match the company's!

Strategy: In your mind, what's the company's strategy? Do you think the company is focused on the right areas? Is there anything that can be improved there?

Strengths: What do you think are the product's selling points? How has the company utilized its strengths to enable its success?

Weaknesses: What are the major issues with the company and/or its products? Should the company change anything to address these weaknesses?

Challenges: What are the biggest current challenges for the company? How are they addressing these challenges?

12 "Our Starbucks Mission Statement," Starbucks Coffee, accessed April 20, 2021, https://en.starbuckscoffee.cz/about-us/our-company/mission-statement.

Opportunities: Do you foresee anything on the horizon that could create an opportunity for the company?

Threats: On the other hand, do you foresee any threats to the company? How would you mitigate these threats?

Future: What do you think the future looks like for this company?

Understanding these business issues and having your own opinions about what they demonstrate and how they can be solved, even if they are not fully formed, will demonstrate business acumen, creative thinking, and confidence in your powers of analysis.

Company Culture

If you ask your interviewer what their favorite thing about the company is, nine times out of ten the answer will be the culture and the people.

Culture is shaped by many different elements: the employees and leaders, the company history and structure, and the environment, which is driven by their values and mission. You should collect as much data as you can about what it would be like to work there day to day. This information should be used not just to impress your interviewers but to also get a feel for the company. Sometimes, candidates can be focused on landing the job and forget to consider if the job is really right for them. It's a two-way street—you have to like them as well!

Saying that, this information is extremely useful at interviews as it demonstrates deep understanding of the company's unique personality as a business. If you can, try to use this information to shape your responses to behavioral or case questions, such as how you would make a go or no-go decision and how that ties in with the company's mission and goals. Let's consider the key areas of research you should be targeting.

Culture: You can find out about the company's culture online by searching through reports about what candidates, current employees, and former employees say about working there. You'll be able to find reviews of the company on the sources mentioned previously (e.g., Blind, Glassdoor), or you could ask around to see if someone you know works for that company and can discuss their experiences with you. You could also check out the company's job page, which should outline their working culture, but that will be biased toward the image the company wants to project.

Mission: A great culture starts with a vision or mission statement. These simple turns of phrase guide a company's values and provide it with purpose. That purpose, in turn, orients every decision employees make. As discussed in the previous section, what's the company's mission statement and values? In other words, what's important to them? I've listed a more detailed discussion about Meta's and Google's missions and values below as an example.

History: When was the company founded? Has the company pivoted at all from its original culture, values, and mission? If so, why? Was this company acquired or merged? Has it acquired other companies? This information might be useful to know because the culture of the company can shift during an acquisition or merger and employees will need to adjust to this cultural shift. For example, after one company buys another, some workers could be deemed redundant and employees may be stressed about layoffs. Employee motivation may drop as frustration with new roles and new coworkers increases. Understanding the company's history can give you a better sense of the culture you should expect.

Interviewers: If you know the names of your interviewers, you can search for them on LinkedIn or social media to find out more. This way, you can already have some questions prepped ahead of time. For example, if your interviewer just graduated from Harvard Business School and mentions that in his introduction, feel free to ask him his thoughts on how useful his MBA is in his current role! You don't want to appear creepy, though, so I recommend you only bring these questions up if it's relevant to something they've said to you.

Key people: Who founded the company? Who are the CEO, COO, and CFO? Who would be at the top of your reporting chain for the position you're applying for? What's the background of the founders or other key people at the company? For example, Sheryl Sandberg was the COO of Meta at the time I interviewed, but she also wrote *Lean In* and *Option B*. I read these books before my interview to get a better understanding of Sheryl's background, values, and personality.

Organization: How big is the company? How's the company organized? Is it flat or hierarchical? If it's flat, they may have a very democratic and less supervised way of making decisions that encourages initiative and involvement in the decision-making process, whereas if it's hierarchical, it may be important to show that you're willing to listen and be led.

Examples of Mission and Values Statements

Mission and values statements can define the reputation of an organization and determine how internal and external stakeholders see them. The following are examples of company missions and values from Meta and Google in 2021:

Meta (previously Facebook)

> **Mission:** "Give people the power to build community and bring the world closer together."
>
> **Values:** Meta's values are (1) be bold, (2) move fast, (3) focus on impact, (4) be open, and (5) build social value. These five values are the signposts that should guide those who work at Meta, and they are core to Meta's culture. During the two-day orientation for new hires, we covered all five of these values. I'll take a deeper look at what these mean in practice and how that shapes what they're looking for in candidates (and, ultimately, how you need to present yourself in the interview).

Be Bold

As Meta's CEO, Mark Zuckerberg, outlined in a letter to investors, "Building great things means taking risks."[13] Within the first few days of orientation at Meta, employees are encouraged to take risks and make mistakes. According to my orientation leader, a Meta intern had tried to push code to production within his first week, but he accidentally created a bug that broke the site and created an outage. However, instead of firing the intern, his team

---

13 Associated Press, "CEO Zuckerberg: Facebook's 5 Core Values," CBS News, May 17, 2012, https://www.cbsnews.com/news/ceo-zuckerberg-facebooks-5-core-values/.

celebrated that he was brave enough to build a new feature so soon into his tenure. Needless to say, that intern got a return offer!

Move Fast

Moving fast allows for faster iterations of products and quick feedback from users. The downside is that moving fast leads to more opportunity for mistakes.

However, even if Meta employees fail, they learn, get up, and continue creating. Meta fosters a culture of builders and learners, and the power is in their hands. In the interview process at Meta, I explained how I would create quick work-in-progress drafts and solicit feedback early on from my stakeholders. That allowed me to incorporate input and continue iterating toward my final product. While this fits in with Meta's values, at other companies it might be better to have a more polished product before sharing with others, so I would shape my approach differently and personalize based on the company and its value statements.

Focus on Impact

At Meta, you'll be rewarded if you can identify and work on the biggest problems. For example, if you've been collecting advertiser insights telling you that the number one issue is lack of reporting capabilities, focus on that first.

The fine balance is figuring out whether to work on the big problem that will take years to solve or the slightly smaller problem that can be solved within a performance review cycle. I and many of my colleagues were guilty of picking the latter because it reflects well on the biannual reviews and ratings.

Be Open

Even from day one, Meta strives to give all employees access to the information they need to do a good job. There is an internal company message board called Workplace that employees can use to search up acronyms, company internal research, and prior presentation decks.

Build Social Value

The point of Meta is to connect the world and create positive change, whether that is through supporting the growth of a local business or building the metaverse for people to connect and explore. Every employee is responsible for contributing to the net value that Meta brings to the society as a whole.

Google

> **Mission:** To organize the world's information and make it universally accessible and useful. Google's aim is to "provide a great service to the world—instantly delivering relevant information on any topic."[14] In 2019, Sundar Pichai, CEO of Alphabet, emphasized a renewed mission to "go from a company that helps people find answers to a company that gets things done."[15]
>
> **Values:** Google is focused on three values: "Respect the user, respect the opportunity, and respect each other." These are posted on the company website.[16]

---

14 Larry Page and Sergey Brin, "Letter from the Founders," *New York Times*, April 29, 2004, https://www.nytimes.com/2004/04/29/business/letter-from-the-founders.html.

15 Sreeraman Thiagarajan, "I/O 2019 Day 1 Highlights: From Finding Answers to Getting Things Done, What's New at Google?" (India) Economic Times, last modified May 8, 2019, https://economictimes.indiatimes.com/magazines/panache/i/o-2019-day-1-highlights-from-finding-answers-to-getting-things-done-whats-new-at-google/articleshow/69228695.cms.

16 Google, "Community Guidelines," accessed January 10, 2022, https://about.google/community-guidelines.

Again, let's look at these in more detail and see how they translate to the working culture.

Respect the User

Users are people, including family members, friends, and neighbors. Some are relying on Google's products to build their company, their clinic, or their nonprofit. Others just need help finding an address. Every one of them is giving Googlers their trust, so Googlers have the responsibility to do right by them.

What does this mean in practice? "Focus on the user."[17] When you think about improving the lives of users, everything else tends to work itself out.

What does this mean during your interview? When you're answering interview questions, don't just think about one archetype of user; expand your thinking to everyone. A problem isn't truly solved if it's only solved for some. As long as barriers like complexity, cost, and access exist, there's still work to do.

Respect the Opportunity

It's a huge responsibility to be able to work on projects that impact billions of people.

What does this mean in practice? Google succeeds when others succeed. Ultimately, Googlers make tools to help others. Small businesses, big enterprises, developers, creators, partners, journalists, teachers, and everyone in between. If they don't succeed, neither does Google.

What does this mean during your interview? Put yourself in the users' shoes. What would you want to see done differently? What are the biggest pain points? Identify the problem with the largest opportunity and then solve it.

---

17 "Google's 10 Core Values," Element 360, November 16, 2015, https://element-360.com/googles10corevalues/.

Respect Each Other

What does this mean in practice? Treat each other with dignity. Each person comes from different places and holds different views, but each Googler has also earned the opportunity to be there.

What does this mean during your interview? You can disagree without being disagreeable. Remember that we're all here to accomplish the same mission. Respectfully listen, debate, decide, and then move forward.

The Role You're Applying For

Last, you should know your role and how it will fit into the company, including why you would be a good fit. This involves understanding the following:

What are your role and responsibilities?

How technical is the role? What percentage of your time involves analysis versus generating insights versus presenting recommendations to leadership? How do decisions get made?

How will you take initiative and make decisions?

Where do ideas come from in the company and how will this impact your approach to decision-making?

Some organizations could have a bottom-up approach to ideation and decision-making, in which ideas bubble up from every level to the executive managers. In this way, the whole organization participates in the process of leading and takes advantage of the "two heads are better than one" approach. The downside is that this is a less agile approach because leadership can't just act on instinct with immediate results.

Other organizations have a top-down approach, wherein ideas and decisions are generated by upper management and passed down the chain of command for carrying out that mission. The downside here is that employees may feel less engaged in their role and the company if they have little power.

Should you favor short-term or long-term thinking?

Some organizations have an appreciation for short-term incremental gains, while others go after the big, bold bets. Ideally, the company will strike a balance between these two extremes. Understanding what the company prefers can help you understand which ideas to pitch.

What would you change about the product?

Come into the interview with ideas for what you'd want to change or improve about the product you'd be working with. Start by understanding some of the major user complaints.

Why do you want the job?

Speak passionately about why you're excited about the company and the strategy or business operations.

Why would you be a good fit?

Make a compelling pitch for how the role matches your skills and background. Beyond just the job description, why are you best suited to tackle the challenges that this company is facing?

You'll definitely learn some of this information at a deeper level during the interview process, but you'll want to walk in with as much information as possible!

The Company's Core Products

You should understand what products are core to the company so that you can be confident when answering interview questions and your enthusiasm will be organic. You will know exactly what you're talking about. You can stand out by knowing the following information:

Products: What array of products or features does the company create? What are the most popular products? How do these products fit in with each other?

Competitors: Who are the competitors? How does the company differentiate itself from the competition? How much market share does your company have? Are you the underdog or the industry leader?

Customers: What's the target market for the company? Are there any secondary markets right now that you'd suggest the company try to enter?

Revenue: What's the primary way the company makes money? What would you suggest the company do to generate more revenue?

Feedback: What do customers love or hate about the product? What are some of the most common issues and complaints? How would you go about addressing these?

Metrics: Take time to get to know the company's key metrics or KPIs (key performance indicators). Although it'll be difficult to find exact numbers on every metric, you can at least get an understanding of which metrics are doing well versus which are not by reading the quarterly earnings reports. How much annual revenue does the company bring in? How many users does it have? What's the growth rate?

News: Have there been any interesting news reports or rumors about the company or industry at large? Don't just read up—formulate your own opinion on it too!

> In order to find this information, check out newspaper articles and see if the company or industry has made any headlines recently or in the past.

Most importantly, you should also use the product yourself before the interview. Ideally, use the product extensively across multiple user personas in order to get a good feel for the variety of experiences that customers might have. If the product has both free and paying users, try to use it in both scenarios. Think about what you liked and what you didn't in each. Ask yourself, if you weren't looking for a job at this company, what would have turned you off about the product?

PART TWO

The BizOps Interview

8

Common Interview Questions

COMPANIES INVEST A LARGE amount of time and resources into the hiring process, whether it's looking through resumes, conducting phone screens, or interviewing candidates. Lots of people are taking time out of their day to get to know you, so please be respectful and make sure you make the most of it by prepping for interview questions. Plus, tech jobs can be competitive, and careful preparation will give you an edge over the competition.

There's a huge range of potential questions you could get asked, but the questions in this chapter come up so often that you'll want to spend extra time preparing for them. I recommend actually rehearsing your answers out loud for each of these questions.

Interview Tips

Interviews can be daunting, and it helps to keep just a few tips in mind that will help you to stay calm and begin with the right mindset. The advice in the next few paragraphs could help you to move from good to great.

Every question in the interview has a *purpose*; they are offering you an opportunity to shine. Think about *why* the interviewer is asking that question so you can effectively tailor your response to show that you're a great future asset for their company.

Everyone rambles when they are nervous. If you can relate, do this: once the interviewer asks a question, pause to think about structuring your answer. For example, briefly outline three core bullet points in your head before you reply.

Many people feel imposter syndrome. Reflect on how your imposter syndrome manifests in interviews (for example, some people don't talk very much, stop asking questions, or have too many ideas). Then, acknowledge what you do when your imposter syndrome kicks in and work toward reducing that type of behavior. For example, if you know that you stop talking, you could write down and memorize bullet points for yourself to help as prompts when you can't think of what to say.

"Tell Me about Yourself" (Your Pitch)

Many interviewers will kick off the conversation with the prompt "Tell me about yourself." In fact, you can almost guarantee that you'll get this question over the course of a full day of interviews. Be prepared to give a solid pitch about your background, accomplishments, and interests that will draw them in and impress.

This is not a time to just read off your resume or go on about your personal life. Instead, pick a few key things you'd like your interviewer to know about you, and use this as an opportunity to connect your experience with the job you're looking for.

Here's my example pitch:

> Interviewer: Tell me about yourself.
> Candidate: Sure thing, I'd be happy to.
> I graduated from Johns Hopkins in 2016 with two degrees in engineering. I originally wanted to go into the medical device industry, but during my senior year, I got an opportunity to build a team of seven people, prototype a device, test it on animals, and then test it on patients. Even after

all this work, it would still take another five to ten years for the device to get FDA approval and launch in the market.

I realized that the medical device industry was a bit slow-paced for me, so I ended up jumping into consulting after graduation. I started at McKinsey in Atlanta, primarily working with banks as my clients. I would gather client, transaction, and account-level data from thirty different banks and create a benchmark to compare their different services. Although I liked the day-to-day work, doing data analysis, meeting with clients, and offering repricing recommendations, I was still missing something. I wasn't able to work on implementation and execution. That became apparent when I would come back to my clients a year later and they would say, "Although we liked your pricing recommendations, we didn't have the resources or team to build out your suggestions." I realized that I wanted to work on the end-to-end aspects of providing high-level strategy as well as helping with implementing solutions, so I started looking into roles in internal consulting or business operations.

I started off on the BizOps team at Groupon, working on product analytics, coming up with recommendations for new product launches, and helping to prioritize the product roadmap. I ended up stepping in as a product manager at some points, leading the development of features like a search bar that hides upon scrolling. At other points, I stepped in as a data scientist, automating a lot of the reporting tools by learning Python and creating weekly business reviews that could be populated by the touch of a button. Unfortunately, Groupon wasn't doing well at the time, so I decided to look for similar roles at other tech companies.

> I'm currently a business operations analyst at Facebook, where I've been for the last two years. I primarily work on revenue forecasting for Newsfeed, which is the largest and most material monetization area at Facebook. My work involves coming up with dollar projections for where the company will be in five years, and I help with coming up with new investment areas and resource allocation decisions. We have four forecasting cycles a year, and although I was learning a lot at the start of my role, I now feel like I've capped out and am not being challenged anymore. I am also stuck doing a lot more operational tasks than I'd like.
>
> Outside of work, I do a bit of coding for fun, sending out automated emails asking for donations and doing web scraping to put together my own grocery lists. I also tutor and mentor high school and college students, and I'm a writer for Lady Gaga's Born This Way Foundation.
>
> I would ideally like to be in a role where I can work on the overall strategy and direction of the company, and I think this role at Google on the acquisitions strategy and operations team will allow me to do just that. I think my prior experience in consulting and analytics will help me ramp up quickly.

In this sample pitch, which I actually used in my Google interview, I walked the interviewer through my background while sprinkling the story with key accomplishments that I could connect together, and then prompted them to ask me more about the areas where I've shined. I formed a cohesive story that explains what I'm good at and why I love being in the BizOps space.

Design your pitch by thinking about what you want the interviewer to know about your background, experiences, and interests. Where possible, connect elements of your pitch to what the company is looking for, as outlined in the job description, whether that's aspects of the role specifically or the company's products and mission statement as a whole.

In addition, keep in mind some of these dos and don'ts:

- *Do* be mindful of how long you speak. Ideally, this should take between one and two minutes. It should be short and focused. Your interviewer will be judging you in part on your communication skills, and nobody likes a rambler.
- *Do* make sure to highlight the interesting and relevant parts of your jobs. Use this opportunity to sell yourself.
- *Do* practice in front of a mirror or record yourself on your phone camera. It's almost guaranteed that you'll be asked for your "pitch," so it would be silly to come unprepared. You will be your own harshest critic, so as cringy as it may be, watch yourself and see what your pitch would sound like on the other side of the table. You could also grab a friend who is willing to be honest and ask for their feedback.
- *Do* use examples instead of talking abstractly. Instead of saying you "analyzed ten thousand rows of data," talk about an example of something important you learned from the data and how you changed or influenced a decision based on that knowledge.
- *Do* be passionate and proud about your previous work.
- *Don't* just list off your accomplishments; tell a story. This could come off as too boastful, and your interviewer may get lost in the details. Instead, you want your pitch to be

a cohesive story about how you got from then to now. It should provide context for why you're a good fit for the role.

- *Don't* talk trash about your previous employer. However reasonable your complaints may be, you could still end up looking petty and disagreeable. Think about how you'd feel if you were on a first date and your new romantic prospect started spouting off about their exes. Wouldn't you prefer them to focus on you and be hopeful for the future rather than stuck in the past? Your prospective employer will feel the same way. No one wants baggage—they want a team player who can show flexibility and adaptability, so make sure to present that image!
- *Don't* get overly technical. It's great if you have some very technical experience, but your interviewer just wants to hear, in straightforward language, why that work was important. After all, as an analyst, you'll be communicating to both technical and non-technical people.

"Why Do You Want to Work Here?"

When I interviewed candidates at Facebook, I'd ask them why they were interested in the position. Many answers would be along the lines of this:

- Facebook has a great culture.
- Facebook has changed the world.
- Lots of people use Facebook products, and I want to work on products that my family and friends use.

While these answers are okay, they don't help you stand out.

Why? Because you haven't given me any information that would make me want to hire you more. Instead, try using your answer to communicate your passion for the role, team, and broader mission of the company.

One way to do this is by weaving in a personal story and incorporating the company's core values or products in your answer. Let's look at an example:

A few years ago, my parents built their own online succulent plant business from scratch. They tapped into the growing popularity of low-maintenance plants and decided to offer one hundred varieties of succulents. I wanted to help them expand their channels beyond their company website to help them reach more potential customers, so I listed their items on Facebook Marketplace. The volume of new orders flooded in and surprised our family, giving our revenues an instant boost of a 66 percent increase. We love that Meta knows how to target the right people. It's helped us reach new audiences we wouldn't have been able to find before.

I want to work at a company that is committed to helping businesses of all sizes grow and create jobs. That's the number one reason why I want to work here! Moreover, I'm excited that I'm interviewing for the strategy role supporting the Marketplace product, because it has made the most impact in my personal life.

You may not have such a unique story to tell, but you can still consider how the product has affected your own life in specific ways and your own personal response to that, whether it's how you relate to your friends and family, how you run your business, or how you buy products.

"Why Should We Hire You?"

This may not be the exact phrasing of the question, but it is often asked, albeit in several different ways. For example, an interviewer might ask why you're a good fit for the role or what you think you can offer to the company.

While this may seem like an intimidating question at first, it is a great opportunity to sell yourself beyond the basic description of how you meet the requirements of the role. Here are some key items you can include in your answer:

Why you're a good analyst and thought partner: Have you shown initiative in your current job? Do you have a good grasp of some technical skills? Have you been successful as a consultant or BizOps analyst in the past? When possible, use specific evidence and examples to back up your answer.

Why you're a good fit for this space: Are you passionate about this space? Why? Have you worked in a relevant area? For example, if you're interviewing for a job at Google or Meta and you know a lot about the advertising space and how advertising auctions work, mention your experience! Advertising makes up the majority of both Google's and Meta's revenue, so it can't hurt to be an expert in that space.

Why you're a good fit for the company's culture: One of Meta's mottos is "Move fast and break things." At Meta, the goal is to ship things quickly and then see what happens in the market. Do you have an example of how you work similarly?

The more familiar you are with the company or position requirements the better. Before your interview rounds, reread the job description and come up with examples for each of the company's minimum and preferred qualifications that will bring your experience to life and make it memorable.

Last, having a structured answer to a fairly open-ended question will not only demonstrate to your interviewer that you're a strong communicator, but it'll also help the interviewer remember the information you give them.

"Why Are You Leaving Your Current Job?"

Your interviewer isn't necessarily looking for anything specific with this question; they just want to learn a bit more about you. However, it's easy to wander into dangerous territory here and leave a bad impression. Your goal should be to avoid raising any red flags.

What topics could screw up your answer?

> **Complaining about your current job or boss:** Interviewers don't like negative candidates, and as they don't know what occurred, they may worry that your dislike of your current role may actually be your own fault. This could put the thought in their mind that you are difficult to please and won't stay in the position.
>
> **Focusing on the money:** A candidate who only cares about making more money doesn't make a great employee. The interviewer may worry that you lack passion and commitment to the job and will be ready to jump ship when an opportunity with more cash comes along.

A better answer focuses on the positive. What are the things you're looking forward to in this new role? You can use any of these as starting points to work into your explanation:

- I'm actually pretty happy with my current role and wasn't actively looking to leave. However, a recruiter reached out to me on LinkedIn and it sounded like a great opportunity that I just couldn't pass up.
- I've had to relocate for personal reasons.

- I enjoy the role itself but I'm not passionate about the product.

- Although I like my current company and day-to-day role, I've been there for several years, and currently, I'm just helping banks make more money. I'd like to be somewhere I can give more back to the world.

"Where Do You See Yourself in Five Years?"

This question might feel daunting, but it can be a great opening for you to demonstrate your commitment to your career and the role itself. The interviewers are asking this question for a few reasons:

- To see if you actually want the job. If this role isn't tied into your long-term goals, it's a red flag to interviewers, and they'll think you're just looking for a short-term job to fill in the gaps. Plus, if you didn't prepare for this question, it might be a sign that you don't really care about the position.

- To see if you have a plan. Successful people tend to have an idea of where they want to go in life. Even if the plan is likely to change, it's better to have a plan than no plan at all. An interviewer may get the sense that you're not serious about your career if you don't have a plan.

- To test ambition. Typically, ambitious people make good employees, as they'll demonstrate commitment, determination, and a drive to succeed. If your long-term goals don't indicate any ambitions, that could be a red flag. Similarly, if your goals are too ambitious and unrealistic, that may not be a good sign either, as it could demonstrate poor judgment.

- To make sure the company can provide what you want. If the role isn't a good fit for your long-term goals, then the company wants to know that. Most likely, you'd be unhappy with your job and quickly leave. That wouldn't be good for anyone, so ideally, you'll have a five-year plan that will align well with the role. Ideally, you want to express expectations that the company would be able to match.

You can also use your answer to highlight what you're good at and what excites you. An example answer to this question might be something like this:

> I'd love to be a strategy and operations manager for an emerging business unit where I can think about long-term strategy, particularly with respect to monetization models. In addition, I'd love to kick-start a formal new employee training program where employees get mentorship and training in different areas of the business.

In this answer, the candidate demonstrated ambition as well as passion for business models, leadership, and mentorship.

"What Do You Like to Do in Your Spare Time?"

This question is mainly used to get to know you and your interests. It can give a better sense of your passions in life, and the best answers will have some sort of relevance to the position. This is also an opportunity for the interviewer to find out whether or not you have drive and ambition, so try your best to share experiences where you can showcase these traits.

Let's look at some *great* example answers that all show some relevance to the job by highlighting the candidate's leadership abilities, technical talent, or initiative. These are all things that make a candidate well suited for a BizOps role.

- I've been spending a lot of time volunteering for a nonprofit organization called the Princess Project. A few months ago, I created a new Silicon Valley chapter, and our mission is to provide free prom dresses and accessories to teens who can't otherwise afford them. Since I started this chapter, we've recruited fifty new volunteers and helped make prom a reality for over two hundred teens.
- I've been interested in learning more about coding, so I recently helped my brother's little league baseball team create an automated script to assign tournament brackets. Now I'm working on my own website!

Now let's look at some *good* example answers. The answers below are solid but don't show any particular relevance to the BizOps role. However, they do show some interests outside of work, and more importantly, they're all backed with concrete evidence and demonstrate ambition, drive, and the ability to follow through.

- I love rock climbing. I climb with some friends after work at Movement in Sunnyvale.
- I enjoy doing construction projects around the house. While I have a lot to learn, I've had a couple of recent successes. I built a fish tank stand and redid the grouting on the shower tiles.
- I enjoy baking on the weekends. Recently, I made my own sourdough starter from scratch! Now I have been feeding it every day and feel a new sense of responsibility.

"What Are Your Strengths and Weaknesses?"

It's likely that, at some point in the interview process, you'll be asked to describe your strengths and weaknesses. This is a question that many job candidates aren't sure how to approach, as listing your strengths can feel boastful and highlighting your weaknesses seems counterintuitive when promoting yourself. However, if you establish the appropriate context, you can give hiring managers an honest and thoughtful assessment that highlights your self-awareness and professionalism.

The key is preparing ahead of time for this question. Even if you're not asked about your strengths and weaknesses specifically, working out a response ahead of time can give you a candid yet compelling description of what you bring to the table and how you want to grow in the future. With this to hand, you'll be able to confidently answer many common interview questions.

The following are example strengths and weaknesses as well as sample answers to help you prepare your response. Examples of strengths include the following:

- Action-oriented or entrepreneurial
- Pays attention to details
- Collaborative
- Committed or dedicated
- Great at communicating
- Creative
- Determined
- Disciplined or focused
- Empathetic
- Enthusiastic or passionate
- Flexible
- Honest
- Innovative

- Patient
- A problem-solver
- Proactive
- Great at prioritization
- Takes accountability

Examples of weaknesses include the following:

- Disorganized
- Critical
- Perfectionism. However, this is a bit overused and many people default to this as a cop-out answer. I've provided two better alternatives:

  » Forgetting to take time to recognize wins and successes, which has led to burnout in the past.

  » Putting too much emphasis on the wrong things, such as obsessing over minor details that have minimal impact on the end result.
- Shy or not adept at public speaking
- Competitive
- Limited experience in a nonessential skill
- Not skilled at delegating tasks or other managerial skills. This is especially useful if you're interviewing for an individual contributor role, as it won't impact on your job prospects but is a good focus for future growth.
- Takes on too much responsibility
- Not detail-oriented

- Too focused or a lack of focus

It can be surprisingly difficult for people to talk about strengths during an interview. During my first job at McKinsey & Company, I was having a one-on-one conversation with my manager and she asked me to list five strengths and five weaknesses. I started off listing my weaknesses and reached all five quite quickly. However, it took me quite a while to come up with any strengths. She ended up listing five strengths for me. Luckily, I already had the job at the time and this was just an exercise to show that I needed more self-confidence.

In the interview, it's a challenge to balance both humility with the need to project confidence. You'll want to use the job description as your guide when you select your strengths. Make sure to follow a framework of (1) listing the strength, (2) adding an example story from your past, and (3) tying this back to why you're qualified for the job and what distinguishes you as a candidate.

> **Example question:** What do you consider to be your two greatest strengths?
>
> **Example answer:** My greatest strengths are that I'm proactive and resourceful. Even if I don't have all the necessary skills before I take on a project, I know that I can learn them and figure it out as I go. For example, I was responsible for creating weekly revenue reviews, and that meant filtering a dashboard and taking screenshots. It was an extremely boring task and took thirty minutes every week for me to take fifty to a hundred screenshots of different cuts of the data and paste them into a slide deck (e.g., slicing revenue by country, by iPhone versus Android, by customer segments, etc.). I took it upon myself to learn Python and automate the creation of this slide deck so that I could press a button and let the script

> create the deck for me while I was grabbing coffee in the morning. This saved me time, and I was able to learn some Python skills and pass on my code to other analysts to save them time on similar tasks.

"What's the Most Recent Book You've Read?"

Some examples of similar interview questions may be, What types of books do you read in your spare time? Do you read any industry publications? If so, which ones? How do you stay current on industry trends? What is your primary way to stay current in your field?

The interviewer is asking this question because they want to find out if you are committed to your career by continuing your personal education in your spare time. If you're engaged in and committed to your career, you will be doing extracurricular reading to stay current.

This question assumes that you read in your spare time (and that you have spare time). Many people do not . . . but don't worry! Now's the time to start. Make sure to focus specifically on reading some books related to your career or industry.

Some examples of books on my reading list are *Hit Refresh* by Satya Nadella, *The Everything Store* by Brad Stone, *Principles* by Ray Dalio, *Elon Musk* by Ashlee Vance, *Made to Stick* by Chip Heath and Dan Heath, and *How Google Works* by Eric Schmidt, Jonathan Rosenberg, and Alan Eagle.

Here's an example of how to best answer this question for experienced candidates:

> **Example answer:** Great question. I'm currently reading a book called *Superforecasting* by Philip Tetlock and Dan Gardner. It explains the methods and personalities of

> superforecasters, people who consistently outperform experts and nonexperts alike in forecasting future events. The book emphasizes the importance of measurement for assessment and revising forecasts and programs. Currently, one of my projects at work is to develop an accurate revenue forecast for Google Cloud. This book has inspired me to track the variance of actuals to the forecast and get constant feedback to iterate and get better.

Here's an example of how to best answer this question for entry-level candidates:

> **Example answer:** Most recently, I've spent a large amount of time reading a study guide in preparation for taking the certification exam for my career. I hope to complete my studies and take the exam before graduation.

In contrast, here's an example of how you should *not* answer this question:

> **Example answer:** Well, I find I don't really have time to read. I try to stay up to date on key developments in the industry via news and my friends, but I don't go further than that.

Outside of books, it's also good to stay up to date with industry news and developments in tech articles. I personally like TechCrunch, and I also subscribe to free email updates from Wing Briefing and StrictlyVC. Wing Briefing (wing.vc/wing-briefing) is a daily curation of the most important news in tech as relevant to corporate executives, founders, and venture investors. StrictlyVC

(strictlyvc.com) is a daily newsletter that provides an overview of the venture capital scene in Silicon Valley and beyond.

"Why Are You Interested in This Role?"

There are a variety of reasons you could provide for why you're interested in the role. I'd focus on preparing three compelling reasons that relate to the responsibilities and potential impact of the position.

Start off by thinking through these questions and writing down your thoughts.

1. When you look at the job description, what excites you?
2. What responsibilities in this role would make you feel fulfilled?
3. What kind of impact do you want to make?

This simple answer structure can be very effective for answering this question: "I'm interested in this role for three reasons. First . . . Second . . . Third . . . Given these reasons, I'd be a great fit for this position."

Here are some example reasons you could give for why you're interested in the role:

- I'd thrive on the high level of autonomy and responsibility that this role offers.
- I'm excited about the potential impact I'd be able to make in this role.
- I'm motivated by challenging tasks and problems that I'd face in this role.
- I enjoy managing a team and developing team members.

- I enjoy collaborating with cross-functional partners.
- I'm passionate about analyzing data and finding insights to drive decision-making.
- I welcome the opportunity to try new tasks with which I have little prior experience (e.g., expanding on my technical skills).
- I feel fulfilled when I get the chance to provide strategic, high-level guidance and recommendations.
- I like solving tangible problems in which I can directly see the impact of my work.

Here are some examples of how you could answer this question using this technique:

> **Example question:** Why are you interested in a strategy and operations role?
>
> **Example answer:** There are three reasons why I'm interested in this strategy and operations role.
>
> First, I enjoy strategic, high-level thinking that drives the direction and roadmap of the company.
>
> Second, I feel energized when I work with different business units within a company. I enjoy collaborating with teammates and cross-functional partners in the pursuit of a common goal.
>
> Third, I'm looking forward to the potential impact that I could make in this role. Not only do my work and recommendations affect the entire company's performance and trajectory, but they could also affect more than two billion users worldwide. Because of these three reasons,

I'm passionate about taking on this role in strategy and operations.

Example question: Why are you interested in an analytics role?

Example answer: There are three reasons I'm interested in this analytics role. First, I enjoy working with a tremendous amount of data. For example, I've regularly worked with SQL data tables with over fifty million rows. I've noticed that I like analyzing data to find critical, actionable insights that are needed to make tough business decisions. Second, I like the autonomy that comes with this specific role. I think it's empowering to own an analysis end to end and figure out where I can add the most value. Third, I feel fulfilled when I'm able to drive impact, and I'm excited to see the difference I'm able to make through my data-driven recommendations. These are three reasons why I believe this analytics role is a great fit for me.

"Why Do You Want to Work in Tech?"

This question is similar to the previous one but a bit broader.

As a starting point, you may want to consider the wider impact of technology and how that makes it an exciting industry. For example, think about (1) how technology impacts billions of people around the world, (2) how technology influences our behaviors in the products we use every day, and (3) how technology solves challenging problems and increases quality of life.

Based on this, here are some reasons you could give for why you're interested in working within the tech space:

- I enjoy working in a fast-paced environment that's continuously changing and evolving.
- I want to work on a product that people enjoy using every day.
- I'm curious about all of the potential use cases of technology in today's world.
- I'd like to play a role in moving the world forward.
- I enjoy the types of challenging problems that tech offers.
- I want to work on products that change and transform people's lives.

Last, connect this interest in tech to the company itself so it underpins your interest in their specific mission and products. Here are some examples of how you might answer this question:

> **Example question:** Why are you interested in tech? (Google)
>
> **Example answer:** I'm interested in tech because it has the potential to improve the quality of life for billions of people around the globe. There's limitless potential for tech to make lives easier, more efficient, and more fulfilling. I'm fascinated by all the different ways tech can benefit society. For example, Google Search has democratized access to information, Google Maps has reshaped the way we navigate the world, and Google Docs has made it possible to collaborate in real time with others on a single document. At Google, I'd be able to contribute my part in moving society forward.

Example question: Why are you interested in tech? (Twitter)

Example answer: I'm interested in tech because it's fast-paced and constantly innovating and evolving. I'd like to be at the forefront of this and tackle the most difficult problems. This includes dealing with fake news, foreign interference in elections, and hate speech, in addition to developers and data privacy. These tough challenges in tech are what gives me excitement and fulfillment in my work. At Twitter, I'd have a unique opportunity to tackle them.

"Do You Have Any Questions for Me?"

As an interview draws to a close, it's almost guaranteed that the interviewer will ask, "Do you have any questions for me?"

When you hear this question, you might groan inside because you feel like you've covered absolutely everything during the previous rounds of interviews and you don't have anything left to discuss. However, it's always better to respond with a question than to politely decline. Otherwise, the interviewer may get the impression that you're not that interested in the position.

Aim to ask open-ended questions and not questions that can be answered with a yes or no. This way, you're giving your interviewer the freedom and space to answer in as much detail as they'd like, without limiting or influencing them with predefined answers. You might find this detail sheds more light on the role than you first anticipate: they may share motivations that you didn't expect or reveal pros and cons of the position that you knew nothing about.

Below are some suggestions for how to respond to this question.

Example Questions about the Role

- Can you share more about the day-to-day responsibilities for this position?
- When would I receive my first performance review? How are these typically conducted?
- In your opinion, what's the single most important trait an analyst in this position should have to be successful?
- How big is the team, and how are the roles and responsibilities split across the team?
- Where does this team fall under the organizational chart?
- Who are the main stakeholders?
- What made you decide to choose this role? (You could turn the tables and ask any of the previously listed questions back at the interviewer: e.g., Why did you choose to work in tech? This may help you gain an understanding of how employees at the company feel about it, relative to yourself.)

Example Questions about the Interviewer

- I'd love to understand a little bit more about your background and how you got to where you are today.
- How long have you been with the company? Have you moved roles or teams since you started?
- What do you think is the greatest challenge the company faces?

- What are some of the company's goals in the upcoming year?
- What made you choose this company over all other options?

Example Questions about Yourself

- Do you have any concerns about my candidacy?
- Are there any qualifications you think I'm missing?

This can be a really good way of finding out a bit more about the employees and company culture too. I often like to ask about something that I've seen in the news or the latest earnings call. If they know *exactly* what I'm talking about, it shows the employees are very engaged in their company, and I generally take this as a good sign. As an example, during my Facebook interview, I mentioned that the latest earnings call mentioned that the company is trying to grow emerging businesses rather than focus on mature areas. I asked, "Given that the company has pivoted focus away from mature areas like Facebook Newsfeed, do you still foresee that I will have impactful work to drive forward as an analyst here?"

The following are some suggestions for topics you should stay away from when asking questions:

Outside-of-work activities and benefits: Asking about happy hours, off-sites, lunch, and vacation time will make it sound like you're not invested in actually doing the work.

Interviewers' personal lives: Give interviewers the same courtesy you'd want them to give to you by not asking about their family, living situation, or gossip about people you may both know. This is a formal, professional situation, and it isn't the time and place, even if you know them.

Things that can be answered online: Don't waste the interviewer's time with questions you can look up the answer to online (e.g., on the company website). The interviewer will expect that you've done your research and already familiarized yourself with the basics.

Salary and compensation: Your salary is typically discussed between you and the recruiter once *all* of the interviews are completed. Try to avoid getting specific about salary and benefits during your interview rounds since that can make you seem more focused on yourself than the work and the company.

Here are some examples of questions that have been asked in interviews that you should *avoid at all costs*:

- How many vacation days do I get?
- How many kids do you have?
- Where does your husband work?
- How much can I expect to earn in my first year?
- Are you pregnant?
- Do you go to church?
- Do you do background checks?
- Are you a native English speaker?

9

Behavioral Questions

SOMETIMES, YOU'LL HAVE A dedicated thirty-to-forty-five-minute behavioral interview. Other times, these types of questions will get sprinkled into your interviews, so it's helpful to prepare even if you don't have a specific "behavioral interview." Behavioral questions are essentially open-ended questions about real-life incidents (often starting with what, how, why, when, and where). They may ask you to share examples of specific situations you've been in and how you've reacted. They may also ask you to elaborate on a particular section of your resume to explain how or why you made a certain decision. Your answers will enable you to use your past work performance to prove what you're capable of doing in the future with this employer.

In the end, they're looking for two elements in how you answer these questions: content and communication.

While it may sound simple, many candidates forget one or both of these factors. They try to come up with any answer that matches the question without focusing on what their answers *say about them* or *how they deliver* the answer.

Your goal is to master both of these factors.

What Are Interviewers Looking For?

Most employers ask behavioral questions because they're considered to be the most effective way to get to know the person behind the resume. The answers to these questions can reveal certain facts about how a candidate has handled real situations that can't be simulated easily in an interview environment. The answers can also help interviewers identify candidates who have the behavioral traits and characteristics that are deemed important for the role.

Research suggests that past behavior is a strong indicator of future behavior and success.[18] These situational interview questions therefore allow employers to gather details that will help them better evaluate applicants and make a strong hiring decision.

How to Prepare for Behavioral Questions

There are a hundred different kinds of behavioral questions you could get asked. Unfortunately, prepping answers for each of the potential variations is neither practical nor feasible. Instead, I recommend an alternative approach that is much more effective and time-efficient.

Prepare five different stories drawn from your prior professional or school experiences. You'll want to select experiences that were the most impactful or unique. Make sure your stories are diverse in terms of what you achieved and what they demonstrated about your skills and personality; you don't want all five of them to be about teamwork. Try to incorporate the following themes: teamwork, leadership, problem-solving, resilience, integrity, influence, and communication. You can also have stories that fit several of these themes. For example, the first story I tell below covers problem-solving, teamwork, and influence.

It's crucial to structure your answers to behavioral questions in order to both keep your stories concise and focus on the key messages you want to convey. The simplest but most effective struc-

18 Karen Franklin, "The Best Predictor of Future Behavior Is . . . Past Behavior," *Psychology Today,* January 2, 2013, https://www.psychologytoday.com/us/blog/witness/201301/the-best-predictor-future-behavior-is-past-behavior.

ture is the STAR method, which is an abbreviation for "situation, task, action, and result." When you're telling your story, you'll want to go through each of these points.

Situation: Give a concise overview of the situation and any context needed to understand the story better. You'll want to answer these questions:

- Who was involved?
- When did this happen?
- Where were you?
- How were you specifically involved?

Example: Last year, I was working at Groupon in their product analytics group. I worked primarily with the mobile product management team, helping to come up with new feature ideas and plan their roadmap.

Task: Describe what you were asked to deliver or achieve. You'll want to answer these questions:

- What were you tasked with?
- What was the goal or objective?
- Why was this task important or necessary?

Example: I was tasked with determining what percentage of our user base was searchers versus browsers and how to convert more users to searchers since searchers spend more money than browsers. This was important because if we could convert more of the user base to searchers, that would provide Groupon with an incremental $10 million in revenue.

Action: Explain the steps you took in order to handle the task or meet your goal. Make sure you focus on what *you* did, specifically, rather than focusing on what your team did. You'll want to answer these questions:

- What steps did you take?
- Why did you decide to take these steps?
- How did you take these steps?

Example: I used SQL and Excel to analyze over one hundred million rows of customer clickstream data points in order to group users into searchers and browsers. Once I figured out that half the users were browsers, I started to brainstorm how we could convert them to searchers. The first answer that came to mind was to increase the size of the search bar a few pixels wider and taller to make it stand out more. I collaborated with product managers, data scientists, designers, and engineers to persuade them to try out this bigger and better search bar. They agreed and we ended up running an A/B test to see if this idea would work.

Result: Describe the outcome of your actions, quantifying the impact and effect you had on the team and company. Last, add your key takeaways from this experience and how that has influenced you as a person. You'll want to answer these questions:

- Did you meet the goal or objectives?
- What was the outcome and impact of your actions?

- What were your learnings from this experience?
- How has this experience helped you grow or develop?

Example: In the end, the A/B test ended up showing statistically significant and negative results for my test, meaning that it failed and I had not met the original objective of creating incremental revenue for Groupon. I was shocked to see that my hypothesis was wrong, so I started digging into the data to understand which of my assumptions were inaccurate. When I went into SQL, I found that the next page type after people clicked into the search bar was primarily NULL, indicating that users bounced. To me, this showed that users who would have browsed got distracted by the new search bar and clicked in, but they didn't know what to do afterward and left. Ultimately, this showed that we can't easily convert browsers into searchers.

Instead, this new insight showed me that we should keep browsers browsing, which is what they do best. I went back to the drawing board and came up with a new idea for a feature: one in which the search bar hides when users start to scroll (indicating browsing behavior). I pitched this new idea to the same team and persuaded them to test this feature out next. We ended up running the A/B test, and this one was finally successful! Once we finished the test, we rolled out the new feature to the entire consumer population, and now, when you open the Groupon app, you'll see a search bar that hides when users scroll.

This experience showed me that user behavior isn't necessarily intuitive, and an A/B test can show vastly different results from your expectations. Luckily, the data will point you in the right direction, so now I try to always use data to inform my product decisions.

Follow-up Questions

Once you've nailed the original question, be prepared for some follow-up questions.

- What was your team's reaction?
- What did you learn from this experience?
- What risks were involved?
- Were you met with any roadblocks or reluctance? If so, what did you do to overcome them?
- What else did you consider prior to taking action?
- Would you do anything differently if this type of situation came up again?
- How does this affect the future of your team?

Types of Behavioral Questions

There are five main categories of behavioral questions that I've been asked before: teamwork, time management, communication, motivation, and leadership. I've listed examples of common questions in each of those categories below.

Teamwork

For questions about teamwork, you want a story that illustrates your ability to work with others under challenging circumstances.

Think team conflict, difficult project constraints, or clashing personalities.

- Tell me about a time you faced a conflict while working on a team. What happened and how did you handle that?
- Tell me about a time you struggled to build a relationship with someone important. How did you overcome that?
- Tell me about a time you wish you'd handled a situation differently with a colleague or teammate.

Time Management

You'll want to prepare yourself to talk about a time you juggled multiple responsibilities, prioritized tasks, and completed everything before the deadline. This could be an example from a previous job, class project, internship, or a sports or volunteer activity.

- Tell me about a time when you had to manage numerous responsibilities or projects. How did you handle that?
- Tell me about a long-term project you managed. How did you keep everything moving along in a timely fashion?
- There are times it's not possible to get everything on your to-do list done. In those situations, how do you prioritize tasks?
- Tell me about a time when your responsibilities got overwhelming. What did you do?

Communication

Communication is not only an important skill in your job; it's important in everyday life as well. Make sure to talk through your thought process and preparation here!

- Tell me about a time when you were able to successfully persuade someone to see things your way at work.
- Tell me about a successful presentation you gave and why you think it was a hit.
- Tell me about a time you had to explain something fairly complex to a client. How did you handle this situation?

Motivation

Seemingly random interview questions may actually be trying to get at what motivates you. Even if the question isn't explicit about it, your response should ideally address this directly.

- Tell me about a time when you worked under close supervision or extremely loose supervision. How did you handle that? What style did you prefer?
- Can you describe a time when you saw an issue and took the initiative to correct it?
- Tell me about your proudest professional accomplishment.
- Tell me about a time when you were dissatisfied in your own work. What could you have done to make it better?

Leadership

People tend to conflate leadership with managing other people, but you can exhibit leadership skills without having a "manager" or "director" title. When probing your leadership skills, your interviewer will be evaluating how you approach your work and get things done, how you take initiative and problem-solve, how you work within a team environment, and the extent to which you've sought to develop yourself and these leadership abilities. Select episodes from your work experience that are specific and really highlight the approach you've taken in these areas.

- Tell me about a time in your current or previous position when you faced a problem that did not have a clear solution. Walk me through what steps you took to overcome this problem.
- Tell me about a decision you made in the last few years that you would change if you could. Why would you choose that one to change? What obstacles did you face? How did you conquer them?
- What approach have you used when providing constructive feedback to coworkers who did not meet your expectations on a project?
- Tell me about a time you implemented a risky approach to reach a goal. Why did you take this approach?
- Tell me about a time when you had to make a tough decision at work in an environment of uncertainty. What was the decision? What was the situation that made the decision tough?
- Imagine you are in charge of delivering a written project report to your supervisor but have never completed one in the past. Your supervisor expects the deliverable by the end of the week. How would you manage this situation?
- Imagine two of your teammates have differing opinions on a project but decisions need to be made immediately. How would you help decide on an approach for the project?

Let's walk through one more example that draws out some

of these themes around time management, communication, and team dynamics:

> **Example question:** Can you tell me about a time you had to work with a difficult stakeholder? What did you do?
>
> **Example answer:** A few months ago, I was working at Google in the strategy and operations team. I was primarily focused on a project to understand if we could use third-party chat platforms (e.g., WeChat, WhatsApp) to better serve advertisers. I was tasked with determining the opportunity size of integrating with a third-party platform, in order to understand if it was worth pursuing despite the legal risks and implications. In order to do this, I needed the marketing team to deliver some numbers for the model. I had a tight timeline and marketing was unresponsive. I tried emailing and then setting up meetings with the team, and although they were willing to meet, this was not a high priority for them so they kept delaying it. I eventually escalated this problem to my manager and he aligned with marketing leadership to make sure both teams were prioritizing this project in the same way. In the end, marketing ended up delivering their numbers on time and I sized out the opportunity to be $100 million. Since this was a significant opportunity, we are currently working with the legal team to negotiate with these third-party platforms. This is a direct result of my work.

10

Case Questions

A CASE QUESTION IS a "hypothetical business situation that is presented during an interview process to determine how a candidate thinks about a particular problem and how they would solve it."[19] These types of questions are typically used in management consulting interview rounds at companies such as McKinsey & Company, Bain & Company, and Boston Consulting Group.

People refer to a "case" as a thirty-to-forty-five-minute exercise in which you and your interviewer work together to develop a recommendation to address and solve a business problem:

- How should Google price its new Pixel phone?
- What can Hulu do to reduce customer churn?
- Should Meta invest in India's largest telecom network, Reliance Jio?
- Which country should Uber expand into next?

At the start of your interview, the interviewer will provide background information and the problem statement. By the end, you'll be expected to present a recommendation and two to three rea-

19 Victor Cheng, "What Is a Case Interview?" CaseInterview.com, July 25, 2020, https://www.caseinterview.com/case-interview-basics.

sons to support your recommendation. In many cases, you'll be presented with charts and graphs and be asked to interpret and analyze them, perform data calculations, brainstorm ideas, and have qualitative insights.

Usually, there's no single right answer for a case. As long as you have logical reasoning and evidence supporting your recommendations, you'll do well.

Even though there are many business problems you could be asked to solve, almost all case questions follow the same structure or format. Thus, you should be able to use the same strategies regardless.

What Are Interviewers Looking For?

Interviewers are looking for you to do the following during a case question:

Clarify the Question

You can't answer a question you don't fully understand. It's important that you make sure you heard the question correctly and truly understand what's being asked.

In your own words, repeat the question back to the interviewer and ask any clarifying question. For example, "Just to make sure I'm understanding the question correctly, you'd like me to evaluate if Meta's Oculus team should enter the video conferencing space and compete with Zoom and Google Meet?"

Structure the Problem

A typical first reaction to hearing a case is "I have no idea where to start." You're given such a broad, big, amorphous problem, and it can be overwhelming! One way to start is by breaking the problem down into three parts:

1. What does the customer want?

2. What do the competitors offer?

3. What should we do about it?

Next time you get stuck, use these three questions as a starting point. If you're on the phone, make sure to list out items. Otherwise, you risk sounding unstructured. For example, "Meta's Oculus team would need to take the following three steps to determine if they should enter the video conferencing space. First . . . Second . . . Third . . ."

Demonstrate Logical Reasoning

In a case question, you'll want to explain your reasoning. It's therefore worth outlining your thought process and the analytical steps that you would go through in answering the question.

For example, if you're consulting Meta's Oculus team, who is looking into expanding into video conferencing, you may say that you'd want to break up the customers into categories. You would begin by asking, "What customer personas are there? What does each category of customer want?"

One customer segment may be using it for work, while another may care only about using this feature with their family. The needs for these two types of personas may be quite different and can change your ultimate recommendation for Meta.

By understanding the full range of customers, you'll be able to better isolate the needs of each segment type and create a recommendation that solves the problem for all these needs.

Analyze the Data

In a case question, you'll want to work through problems in a numerical way. For example, you could look at the percentage of the overall market that each segment represents. Do business-heavy users make up 1 percent of the market or 99 percent? That could have a huge impact on what your client should do.

Another part of analytical reasoning involves looking at direction of change. If this business-heavy customer base makes up only 1 percent of the marketplace, is it growing? Is it becoming a more or less favorable base to target?

Synthesize and Communicate Your Conclusions

There's a major difference between a summary and a synthesis. A summary is a restatement of facts. Synthesis means digesting those facts and using them to develop an insight into what the client should do and why.

Make sure you synthesize by stating your findings and creating an insight with action-based recommendations in a way that is very client friendly. Some things you may want to consider are the company's strengths and weaknesses, the state of the current and future market, and pros and cons of your recommendation.

For example, your synthesis could be something along the lines of this:

> I recommend that Meta's Oculus team expand their virtual reality tools into the next generation of video conference calls. VR conferencing's benefits like interactivity, immersion, and a distraction-free environment are currently untapped by current communication tools. Meta should be at the forefront of creating this experience, as it fits with the company's mission of building community and bringing the world closer together. Moreover, the Oculus team already has the best-in-class hardware and technology to leverage for this use case. Finally, the data supports this recommendation. Based on survey data, business-heavy users currently make up 60 percent of the market, and this share continues to grow, year over year.

Remote work is on the rise and the need for a more immersive video conferencing experience is crucial now and in the future.

Framework Area	Notes Area

Useful Frameworks for Solving Case Questions

Frameworks are there to give you a suggested structure for a problem or point you to an area you might otherwise have missed. However, don't make the mistake of whipping out frameworks left, right, and center and trying to force fit them into the problem at hand. Structure matters! Memorizing frameworks doesn't.

While the interviewer is giving you the case background information, start taking notes. Turn your paper landscape and draw a vertical line to divide your paper into a "Framework" section and a "Notes" section.

When you start to hear a case question, think about how you can break it into smaller questions to make it more manageable. Frameworks provide a systematized way of approaching common business problems. They can help you to take a big and complicated problem and dismantle it into its component parts. Typically, frameworks should have three to five subsections, also known as "buckets," that support this process. I've outlined some frameworks as examples:

Customer Purchase Funnel Framework

The most popular framework for modeling the customer funnel is the AIDA model for marketing and advertising. The four steps for AIDA represent stages of the marketing campaign that the consumer must go through to become a customer. An example of a case question where this might be useful is "Which stage of the customer purchase journey should our company focus on? Where is the largest drop-off in customers, and how does it compare to our competitors?"

In the AIDA model, each consumer must pass through one stage to proceed to the next:

Attention: The first step is getting the consumer's attention. This could be a shocking heading, a personalized advert, or an intriguing photo.

Interest: Once you have the consumer's attention, you want them to become interested in your offering. What are the benefits of your product?

Desire: After you have their interest piqued, you need to convince them that they can't live without your product.

Action: Last, you'll want the consumer to take action to purchase your product. This could be a final reminder to call, visit the website, or take advantage of a sale, inspiring consumer action. Making sure your "ordering system is as easy to use as possible helps promote seamless action by your newfound customers" as well.[20]

20 Kristien Matelski, "The AIDA (Attention, Interest, Desire, Action) Formula," Vizion, April 16, 2019, https://www.vizion.com/blog/the-aida-attention-interest-desire-action-formula/.

The Four Ps of Marketing

This framework is called the four Ps and is a way to understand different elements of a marketing plan for a new or existing product. An example question this might be useful for is "How should we price and market the new product we're launching?"

Product: This is the item being offered, and it should cater to the customer's wants and needs.

Price: The price is determined by how many and what kind of customers want to purchase the product. Generally, three different approaches are used to set the price of a product:

1. Cost-based pricing
2. Competitive analysis
3. Value-based pricing

The "right" price is the one that maximizes the revenue. To sell the greatest amount at the best price possible, we need to know how people value the product; therefore, value-based pricing is usually recommended.

Promotion: Promotions include all forms of advertising, PR, and word of mouth.

Place: For online products, this "place" could be a website. For physical products, it could include things like online sales through Amazon, opening brick and mortar stores, distribution through other retail stores, and so on.

SWOT Analysis

SWOT analysis, using a two-by-two matrix, is one way to analyze companies and products, and it's a simple but effective tool to develop business strategy. You can employ a SWOT analysis "before you commit to any sort of company action, whether you are exploring new initiatives, revamping internal policies, considering opportunities to pivot, or altering a plan midway through its execution." In this way, it's very flexible as a framework.[21] An example case question that this could be useful for is "Should we consider a merger, acquisition, or joint venture with [another company name]?"

Strengths: Strengths are the internal factors that could benefit the product: costs, company reputation, infrastructure, features, or other aspects.

Weaknesses: Weaknesses are internal factors that introduce challenges to the product: no online reviews or brand presence, high-maintenance costs compared to its competitors', lack of expertise in digital marketing, or gaps in other capabilities.

Opportunities: Opportunities are focused on external factors like competition, market growth, technology changes, and regulations.

Threats: Threats are external factors such as the competition holding majority market share, innovation on the market that will make your product outdated, or other trends that could negatively affect your business.

21 Skye Schooley, "SWOT Analysis: What It Is and When to Use It," Business News Daily, last modified December 1, 2021, https://www.businessnewsdaily.com/4245-swot-analysis.html.

The Five Cs of Strategic Marketing

These five Cs can guide a decision on whether to launch a new product and what the strategy should be. An example of a relevant question is "What are the strengths and weaknesses of our company's brand? What are your suggestions for actionable marketing strategies we should undertake in the next six months?"

Company: This covers all aspects of a company, including its products, culture, strengths, weaknesses, brand reputation, and infrastructure. What are key characteristics that define your company?

Competitors: These could be direct competitors, potential competitors, or substitute products. Who is standing in your way?

Customers: This includes aspects like purchase behavior, market size, channels for distribution, and customer wants and needs. Who are you selling to?

Collaborators: These could include suppliers, distributors, or partnerships in general. Who would you work with and how would they enable success?

Climate: This includes regulations, tech changes, economic environment, and any cultural trends. What are the current business conditions?

Porter's Five Forces

This framework considers the five forces that affect the competitive position of a company. It's useful for assessing and evaluating the strength of a business organization and the threats to that strength. For example, if the interviewer asked you to evaluate Apple's position in the technology sector, you could do that with this framework, as I'll outline.

Buyer power: Depending on the number of buyers and their share of revenue, some buyers could have significant power. This would allow them to drive prices down, affect delivery timelines, and dictate terms. With the Apple example, the individual buyer power is small since the loss of any one customer represents a negligible amount of revenue for Apple. However, the collective marketplace bargaining power of customers and the possibility of mass customer defections is a strong force. Apple is able to manage this force by continuing to develop new and unique products like AirPods and the Apple Watch, building significant brand loyalty and establishing a large customer base that would not consider abandoning the Apple ecosystem of products.

Supplier power: Similar to buyers, suppliers can drive up prices. This is determined by the number of suppliers, uniqueness of their product or service, relative size and strength of the supplier, and cost of switching from one supplier to another. Since Apple has a large number of potential suppliers for component parts, the bargaining power of suppliers is a relatively weak force. The cost of switching from one supplier to another is also not an obstacle.

Competitive rivalry: The number and capability of competitors in the market can drive prices up or down. If there are many competitors offering undifferentiated products and services, that will generally drive down prices for everyone. The competitive rivalry for Apple is high since they are competing with Google, Samsung, Amazon, and Hewlett-Packard, just to name a few. All these companies expend significant capital on research and development (R & D) as well as marketing. The other thing to note here is that there are low switching costs for the customer. It doesn't require significant investment for the consumer to ditch Apple's iPad for an Amazon Kindle or something similar.

Threat of substitution: Competition exists not only from direct competitors but also from substitute products. When substitute products exist in the market, it increases the likelihood of customers switching to alternatives in response to price increases. This would lower both the power of suppliers and the attractiveness of the market. In the case of Apple, a landline phone might be a substitute for owning an iPhone. However, this market force is low as the potential substitute products have limited capabilities compared to Apple's products.

Threat of new entry: New entrants are attracted to profitable markets, and that means more competition. Unless existing companies have strong and durable barriers to entry (for example, proprietary technology, economies of scale, a strong brand, or government policies that protect them), then profitability will decline to a competitive rate. For Apple's market share, the threat of a new entrant to the marketplace is relatively low. This is because (1) a massive amount of capital would need to be spent on R & D and manufacturing in order to develop and produce a product portfolio that could compete with the existing products on the market and begin to generate revenue, and (2) Apple and its major competitors have very strong brand recognition, and it would thus take a lot of time for a new entrant to establish this kind of trust and awareness within the industry.

It could also be argued that governments are a sixth force for many industries since they determine regulation, taxation, and trade policies. With the Apple Watch Series 4 and beyond, for example, an ECG function is enabled in some countries but is not yet internationally available. This is because ECG is considered to be a medical device, and some governments have not given clearance to allow Apple to enable this feature.

Create Your Own

While these frameworks can be a good starting point for analyzing a problem, more often than not you'll need to create your own strategy for the problem at hand. In the actual interview, you may need to tweak one of these frameworks or blend some together to find the perfect solution.

Types of Case Questions

Before your interview, you should conduct thorough company research (review chapter 7 for information sources) to ensure you are fully prepared to answer case questions.

These are six of the most common types of questions you'll get:

1. **Company performance questions:** What is the company's competitive advantage? What are they doing well versus what are they doing poorly?

2. **Growth questions:** What markets or customers should the company acquire?

3. **Competition questions:** Who are the main competitors? What differentiates this company from the competition?

4. **Risks and threats questions:** What are the biggest risks and threats to the company?

5. **Trends questions:** What are the major trends over

time? What levers does the company have to respond to these trends?

6. **Estimation questions:** Through estimation, what's the revenue opportunity and costs for a certain product within this company?

Let's look at each of these in more detail.

Company Performance Questions

You should go into the interview having some perspective on the company's competitive advantage. Does it come from customers having a higher willingness to pay? Does it come from a lower product cost compared to other competitors?

There are plenty of reasons why their customers may have a higher willingness to pay. Perhaps the product is superior to others in the market (faster, more durable, easier to learn), or there's a brand name attached that people are willing to pay a premium for. Or it could be that this product has synergies with other products that these customers value. For example, Apple is a premium brand and the products tend to link together seamlessly, making existing customers more likely to buy several devices from the company rather than venture into other brands.

There is also a multitude of reasons why the company might have lower costs to produce. Perhaps the company is large enough in scale to negotiate lower prices with suppliers or has the technical knowledge needed to lower costs with more efficient design and production.

Identifying the company's competitive advantage and detailing the reasons why will help you reveal the company's strengths and weaknesses. Strengths help the company achieve its competitive advantage. Weaknesses put the company's competitive advantage at risk.

Growth Questions

Take some time to think about how the company can grow, both organically and inorganically. You can think about organic growth as the revenue that a company can achieve by increasing its output and enhancing sales. Meanwhile, inorganic growth is growth through acquisitions or partnerships, which bring in revenue and profit from an external party.

Within organic growth, you can break it into existing revenue streams and look at techniques to maximize profit, including repricing, increasing sales effectiveness, cross-selling, upselling, and entering new markets or customer segments. Or you could consider new revenue streams (i.e., developing new products and services). Within inorganic growth, you could look at the potential to either acquire relevant companies or partner with them.

When you form a perspective on how a company should grow, make sure to consider all these various avenues.

The growth pathways framework below summarizes the different opportunities for growth:

- Organic growth:
    - » Growth from existing revenue streams
        - ◊ Repricing
        - ◊ Increasing sales effectiveness
        - ◊ Cross-selling
        - ◊ Upselling
        - ◊ Entering new markets
        - ◊ Pursuing new customer segments
    - » Growth from new revenue streams
        - ◊ Launching new products
        - ◊ Launching new services

- Inorganic growth:
    - » Acquiring a company
    - » Partnering with a company

Competition Questions

You should have a view on how the company's competitors are performing, as this sheds light on their competitive advantage, strengths and weaknesses, and risks and threats to their position. First, identify the competitive advantages that other players have. This advantage comes from either having a higher customer willingness to pay or having a lower cost to produce compared to other players.

Then, compare the competitive advantage of the company with the competitive advantage of other players in the market. How can they sustain their competitive advantage over others and vice versa?

Any competitors that have products that directly compete or are substitutes can be considered a threat.

Risks and Threats Questions

Outside of competition, you should have a perspective on the largest risks to the company. These risks could be either internal or external to the company. Internal risks include product risk, execution risk, and team risk. External risks are primarily market risk.

Product risk is the possibility that the product or service will fail to satisfy customer expectations. Execution risk is the possibility that the company fails to put the business plan into action. Team risk is the possibility that management will fail to work together effectively. Last, market risk is the possibility that regulations, technologies, or customer needs will change. This last subset of risks creates uncertainties that the company has limited control over. For example, in July 2021, the Chinese government cracked down on the popular ride-hailing provider Didi.[22] The local regulators announced a cybersecurity review of the company and ordered Didi to block new user signups in the meantime. Didi had limited control over this external factor and took a significant hit to revenue after just having gone public.

Trends Questions

Finally, make sure you have a perspective on how major trends impact the company and what they should do in response. These trends could include customer trends, competitor trends, and market trends. You'll be able to find analysis of these trends in annual reports from sources such as Bain & Company, Deloitte, Salesforce, and CB Insights.

Customer trends change based on customer preferences, needs, behaviors, and purchasing habits. For example, the COVID-19 crisis changed how consumers behaved at work. More consumers needed to work remotely, and the number of Zoom's daily participants increased twentyfold.[23] What do you think Zoom had to do in order to adapt to these changes?

Competitor trends reflect what other brands are doing in product development, marketing, supplier sourcing, and overall strategy. What are competitors doing that the company should pay attention to?

Market trends change based on new technologies and regula-

---

22 Alex Wilhelm, "Chinese Cybersecurity Probe Validates Didi's Pre-IPO Warning to Investors," TechCrunch, July 2, 2021, https://techcrunch.com/2021/07/02/chinese-cybersecurity-probe-validates-didis-pre-ipo-warning-to-investors/.

23 Sajal Kohli et al., "How COVID-19 Is Changing Consumer Behavior—Now and Forever," McKinsey & Company, June 2020, https://www.mckinsey.com/~/media/mckinsey/industries/retail/our%20insights/how%20covid%2019%20is%20changing%20consumer%20behavior%20now%20and%20forever/how-covid-19-is-changing-consumer-behaviornow-and-forever.pdf.

tions. Which areas would you recommend the company invest in based on these market changes?

Estimation Questions

Examples of estimation questions might be:

- How much revenue does YouTube make per day?
- How many Uber drivers are there in the US?
- How many restaurant reviews are written on Google Reviews every month?

Estimation questions can be intimidating at first, but it's important to keep in mind that it's *how* you answer rather than *what* you answer. The purpose of these questions is to analyze how you approach a problem. Do you get frustrated when you don't understand a problem? Do you jump right into a problem without asking clarifying questions? These would be examples of red flags for the interviewer.

North America population	400 million
World population	8 billion
World population with internet access	5 billion
Europe population	800 million
Asia population	4 billion

For estimation questions, it's useful to develop a bit of intuition about numbers and to memorize a few key ones. Here's a brief cheat sheet you can use for estimation or sizing questions.[24] Note that these are 2021 numbers:

24 "Internet Usage Statistics," Internet World Stats, March 31, 2021, https://www.internetworldstats.com/stats.htm.

Example question: What's Gmail's revenue from advertising in a year?

Example answer: You'll need to make a lot of assumptions here, but they are looking to observe how you approach a problem rather than how close you get to an accurate response. I'll walk you through what I feel is a reasoned answer:

Number of active 30-day users (this is the total number of users who log in and engage with the product over a period of 30 days):

- People in world population who have internet access: 5 billion.
- Gmail penetration is high in North America and Europe (most people I know in these areas have Gmail accounts). Let's assume 60% penetration using the numbers in the table above, so 60% of (400m + 800m) = 720m active Gmail users.
- Let's assume that the rest of the world with internet access (4.3b) has low Gmail usage of around 10% = 430m. That brings the total to 720m + 430m = 1.2b active Gmail users.

Impressions:

- Let's assume the typical user sees 3 ad impressions (at the top of the inbox tabs and other places). This means 1.2b Gmail users × 3 ad impressions per user = 3.6b impressions.
- Click-through rate (CTR), which is clicks / impressions: For targeted email advertising, typically the CTR is 2–5%. Since the ads I see in Gmail are only loosely targeted, we'll say 2% CTR for Gmail.

- Revenue per ad: Since loosely targeted ads don't pay very much, let's assume these are $0.5 per click. This is based on my previous experience when I've dogfooded ads (meaning these are results from my own internal beta testing of ads).

  Now for some math:

- 3.6b impressions per month × 2% CTR = 72m clicks per month
- 72m clicks per month × $0.5 revenue per click = $36m per month
- $36m per month × 12 months = $432m per year

Once you've walked through the math, you should also do a sanity check! Keep in the back of your mind that Google makes $180b a year in revenue. Since Gmail is likely to be a small part of that, $432m could be in the right ballpark.

Remember that your final outcome of $432m is not what matters. Your interviewer cares more about your overall approach to the problem, and you can still ace this question even if you don't get to the right answer. The most important part is making sure you have sound logic and communication skills.

An Example of a Case Question and Answer

Below is a BizOps interview case question and example answer that explores raising the price of Amazon Prime. It's broken into three prompts that tackle different elements of the business problem. You'll see that several of the topics we discussed earlier are incorporated into this line of questioning.

Prompt 1

Amazon is considering increasing the price of Amazon Prime from its current $99 per year. You are being asked to investigate whether a price increase is a good idea. How would you evaluate this decision?

Answer 1

I suggest we evaluate (1) direct Prime revenue, (2) indirect Prime revenue (i.e., what Prime customers spend via Amazon), and (3) costs associated with Amazon Prime.

A price increase would likely have an impact on revenue generated directly from Amazon Prime: Number of Prime customers × Prime subscription fee per customer = direct Prime revenue.

It's also likely to impact incremental revenue generated indirectly from customers using Amazon Prime: Number of Prime customers × (Amazon goods revenue per Prime customer – Amazon goods revenue per non-Prime customer) = Incremental goods revenue attributable to Amazon Prime.

Additionally, this could impact margin via costs. The margin is lower on each Prime order due to higher shipping costs borne by Amazon (since Prime users can get free two-day shipping). Therefore, the possible decrease in Prime members motivated by the price increase could potentially improve the company's margins even if Prime membership fees are lost because the overall number of customers requiring free delivery will reduce.

Prompt 2

Amazon is focused only on the revenue implications of this price increase and not on cost implications. What would you do next to evaluate whether the price increase will increase revenue?

Answer 2

First, I would evaluate direct Prime revenue: How would the number of customers change with a price increase?

Data sources:

- Results of past price increases
- Quantitative and qualitative surveys
- Comparable products
- A/B tests in market

Next, I would look at indirect Prime revenue: How much do Prime customers spend versus non-Prime customers?

Data source:

- Internal spend data around Prime versus non-Prime customers

Ideally, I'd segment internal spend data into customers likely to be retained despite a price increase versus customers likely to churn with price increase (retained customers would likely have a higher average goods spend). Some companies will have propensity models to predict customer behavior like this.

Prompt 3

Given data on the variables above, how would you set up a simple equation to determine whether the Prime price increase would be revenue positive?

Answer 3

In order to set up a simple equation to determine whether the

Prime price increase will be revenue positive, I'll assume the following:

- Prime membership fee: \$99 → \$129
- Number of Prime members: 80m → 78m
- Annual goods spend:
  - » Retained member: \$1,000
  - » Lost member: \$500
- Current state:
  - » Number of current Prime members × (Prime membership fee + annual goods spend) = Total annual revenue from Prime
  - » 80m × (\$99 + \$1,000) = ~\$88.0b from Prime members
- Comparison state:
  - » Number of new Prime members × (new Prime membership fee × annual goods spend) = Total annual revenue from new Prime members
  - » 78m × (\$129 + \$1,000) = ~\$88.1b from Prime members
  - » And then add \$500 × 2m = \$1b from non-Prime members (assuming you would still get their Amazon goods spend but not their Prime revenue)
  - » Thus, the comparison state is \$88.1b + \$1b = \$89.1b

The Prime price increase will therefore be revenue positive by approximately \$1.1b.

Prompt 4

What would you do to improve upon this analysis?

Answer 4

In order to improve upon this analysis, I'd look at two additional factors:

The first is the sensitivities of all the key variables of this analysis, as shifts in key variables could shift the answer. For example, it might be that the shift in price from $99 to $129 would result in a greater loss in number of Prime users than what I've assumed here (–2m). If so, that could change my answer. In order to do a comprehensive analysis, I would assume a worst-, medium-, and best-case scenario to make sure I cover all the bases.

I'd look at the impact of a price increase on the growth of Prime members over time and their spend. This analysis is currently static, but I would change it into a forecast model.

* * *

The reason this is a good example of a case question is because this would be the type of real-world business problem that a strategy team at Amazon would work on. Pricing case questions are very common, and the answers here show that the interviewee has created a mutually exclusive, collectively exhaustive (MECE) framework of revenue and costs, can work through the math, and can come up with a strong recommendation for the team. The interviewer would likely receive this well, as the answers show a clear understanding that the candidate can problem-solve and communicate succinctly about why the team should increase the price of Prime. These are the techniques and level of insight you can apply to different case questions going forward.

11

Technical Questions: Analytical Tools Such as SQL

When you apply for an analyst position in BizOps, it is likely you'll also have to answer technical questions to demonstrate your knowledge of data analysis and show that you're self-sufficient. No matter which product or service you work on, data will be an integral part of your role, and all this information is stored in a database in the form of data signals and attributes. Technical questions may require specific knowledge of analytical tools such as SQL, Python, R, MATLAB, or Tableau. Think of these tools as a shortcut to the data.

Make sure you are familiar with the data and analytics tools listed in the job description. If you haven't used these tools before, you'll likely want to learn the basics before your interview. SQL is prevalent in the field and frequently tested on in interviews, so I'll dive deeper into SQL specifically in this chapter.

Do I Need to Know How to Code?

This is the question you're likely asking yourself. The good news is that you don't need to be an expert coder to thrive in BizOps, but understanding the basics of coding can allow you to self-serve and have a deeper understanding of the data. Doing this will help you not only retrieve data but also better interpret the data you'll need to inform business decisions. With the rise of the cloud and big data, it's no longer feasible to just complete analyses in Excel. You'll likely need to start working with multiple and larger datasets where you need more powerful tools like SQL (Structured Querying Language).

SQL is an extremely desirable skill for anyone in today's marketplace, and it's increasingly common for employers to require at least a basic knowledge of SQL in professions related to business analytics, finance, statistics, banking, and data science.

If you're completely new to SQL, I recommend checking out W3 Schools (w3schools.com/sql/default.asp). This is my favorite free online resource, and it has a lot of great examples and "try it yourself" features that allow you to practice writing sample SQL scripts. Another fun resource is HackerRank (hackerrank.com/domains/sql), which allows you to practice basic, intermediate, and advanced levels of SQL through programming challenges. With each challenge, you accrue points based on answer accuracy, and HackerRank will update the world leaderboard to show you where your score ranks versus other players.

Common SQL Questions and Example Answers

Let's look at some commonly asked SQL interview questions for business analyst or strategist positions to give you some insight into the level of knowledge an interviewer would be expecting.[25]

Question: What is SQL?

Answer: SQL stands for Structured Query Language and is used to store and retrieve data.

Question: What are aggregate functions?

25 Dorata Wdzięczna, "Most Popular SQL Interview Questions for Business Analysts," Learn SQL, October 25, 2017, https://learnsql.com/blog/popular-sql-interview-questions-business-analysts/.

Answer: Aggregate functions allow you to consolidate rows of the data and perform calculations to create a single row. Some common aggregate functions include:

- AVG calculates the average of the column and returns a single row.
- COUNT calculates the number of rows in the column and returns a single row.
- MAX calculates the max of the column and returns a single row.
- MIN calculates the min of the column and returns a single row.
- SUM calculates the sum total of the column and returns a single row.

Question: What's the purpose of the GROUP BY statement?

Answer: The GROUP BY statement is used to summarize information into groups. For example, if there is a GROUP BY REGION, then all the "US" rows will get consolidated into one "US" row. GROUP BYs are typically used in conjunction with aggregate functions.

Question: What is an INNER JOIN?

Answer: INNER JOIN combines two tables and only keeps the rows that completely overlap.

Question: What's the difference between a LEFT JOIN versus a RIGHT JOIN?

Answer: A LEFT JOIN takes all the rows from the left

table, regardless if they match the table joined on the right side. LEFT JOIN is also known as LEFT OUTER JOIN. Meanwhile, RIGHT JOIN only takes the rows from the table on the right.

Question: In what situations should you use WHERE and HAVING in a statement?

Answer: WHERE is used to filter rows of data, whereas HAVING is used to filter out an aggregate group. For example, you could write WHERE date = '2020-01-01' to filter to that date specifically, and you could write HAVING sum(revenue) > $0 to filter the aggregate of the sum of revenue.

Question: What function can you use to get non-repeated values?

Answer: The DISTINCT function can be used to return only the unique values for a particular column or expression.

Question: What does the IN function do?

Answer: The IN function can be used in conjunction with the WHERE clause to specify multiple values. For example, your SQL syntax could be "WHERE region IN ('APAC', 'EMEA')."

Question: What is a subquery?

Answer: A subquery is a query nested inside another query. This inner query will run before the outer query, and the results will get passed on accordingly.

Once you get through basic questions, you may be asked to write some SQL queries on a whiteboard in response to a theoretical scenario. The following are two examples of SQL interview whiteboard questions. Please note that there are multiple ways to get to a correct answer, and yours doesn't need to match mine exactly. The best way to practice is to create sample tables and test your query on them to make sure you get the answer you expect.

Question 1

Let's say you have two SQL tables: authors and books. The authors dataset has more than one million rows. Here are the first six rows:

author_name	book_name
author_1	book_1
author_1	book_2
author_2	book_3
author_2	book_4
author_3	book_5
....	....

The books dataset also has more than one million rows, and here are the first six. Based on both tables, create a SQL query that shows the top three authors who sold the most books in total.

book_name	sold_copies
book_1	1000
book_2	1500
book_3	34000
book_4	29000
book_5	4000
....	....

Answer

```
SELECT author_name
FROM
(SELECT author_name, SUM(sold_copies) as Total_Sales
FROM authors a
JOIN books b ON a.book_name = b.book_name
GROUP BY author_name
ORDER BY 2 DESC
LIMIT 3) c
```

First, I'm selecting the total number of sold copies by author. By ordering the list descending and limiting to only three rows of data, I've filtered to only the top three authors. Then, because the question only asks for the author names and not their book sale numbers, I've only selected author_name on the outside of the parenthesis.

Question 2

Let's say you work for a company that makes online presentation software. There's an event log that records every time a user inserts an image into a presentation. (One user can insert multiple images.)

The event_log SQL table looks like this, and it has over one billion rows:

user_id	event_date_time
123456	153530842
123456	153530848
147515	153530862
694672	153530894
694672	153530895
694672	153530932
....	....

Write a SQL query to find out how many users inserted more than 1,000 but fewer than 2,000 images in their presentations.

Answer

```
SELECT COUNT(user_id) AS user_count
FROM (SELECT user_id
FROM event_log
GROUP BY user_id
HAVING COUNT(event_date_time) > 1000 and
COUNT(event_date_time) < 2000) t;
```

First, I've selected the user IDs that have more than 1,000 but fewer than 2,000 timestamps for events. Since each timestamp represents an image insertion, I've effectively limited the search to the users that have inserted more than 1,000 but fewer than 2,000 images into their presentations. Then, on the outside query, I'm counting the number of users to answer the question of how many users inserted more than 1,000 but fewer than 2,000 images in their presentations.

What Are Interviewers Looking for?

Evaluation of your performance isn't about whether you got the right answer or not. Rather, the evaluation is a lot more qualitative and subjective. The interviewer wants to know how you go about problem-solving.

They will be looking for the following:

- How did you start tackling the problem? A good start is repeating back the question in your own words to make sure you understand the problem correctly.
- How willing were you to solve the problem? If you seem willing to give up right away, that can be a red flag. Inter-

viewers want candidates who are excited about solving tough problems since those people tend to make good employees.

- How quickly did you solve it? If you solved it quickly and correctly, the interviewer will be impressed! If you solved it slowly but correctly, that's also good, but it could indicate to the interviewer that you may need longer timelines for a project.

- How efficient was your approach? There are typically many ways to solve a problem, but if your method was more efficient, that'll garner you more points with the interviewer.

- How much help did you need? If you needed handholding from the interviewer to get to all the answers, then that's a red flag. Interviewers are looking for someone who can independently solve problems and only ask for help when necessary.

- How was your communication when discussing the problem? Talking out loud is helpful and allows your interviewer to tell when you're getting stuck and provide input.

- How did you react to feedback and guidance from your interviewer? If you're silent when going through your work and then you get the wrong answer, your interviewer can't even give you partial credit for your reasoning and thought process.

None of your answers to these questions will lead to a definitive yes or no when it comes to getting the job. Instead, your interviewer will be comparing your answers indirectly with other candidates to get a feel for your relative potential. The first time they ask a question, they won't know whether a candidate's response is fast or slow. However, as they ask more and more people the same question, it becomes clearer. If most people took twenty to thirty minutes to solve a problem and you get it in ten minutes, they'll know you solved it quickly. Since the evaluation is relative, it's difficult to judge by yourself how you did in an interview. You may feel that you struggled, but you don't know how much the other candidates struggled in comparison.

Common Mistakes to Avoid

Let's consider a scenario when you have to code in the interview. Oh no, you run into an error when you try to run your script! The most important thing is to not panic. This isn't uncommon and can often be resolved. Here are some common SQL mistakes to look out for when you're practicing or interviewing:

- An open parenthesis somewhere (like an "IN" clause).
- Wrong cases: table names and field names are case sensitive; syntax is not.
- Commas needed between fields in your select statement.
- Forgetting to group by all your non-aggregate fields.
- Not using prefixes in your select statement when pulling from multiple tables.
- Forgetting to define aliases for your tables when using joins.
- Forgetting the "ON" clause in a join.
- Clauses out of order: has to be SELECT, FROM, WHERE, GROUP BY, ORDER BY.
- Trying to join on different data types (e.g., a string with a date).

Picking up a new language like SQL can be frustrating, so don't be too hard on yourself. Celebrate your successes, even minor ones! Just know that the key to your success is moving forward each day and not giving up. Any skill takes time to learn and more time to master. Be persistent.

12

The Take-Home Challenge

OCCASIONALLY, YOU'LL GET A take-home assignment in which the interviewer gives you a sample dataset and a business question to answer. You'll analyze and interpret the data and make presentation slides to communicate your findings.

You should expect a deadline to complete the data challenge. Typically, once the interviewer sends you the dataset, you'll have between one and seven days to complete it. Make sure you clarify what the turnaround timeline is with the interviewer.

Most of the time, the dataset is sent in Microsoft Excel format, and you'll be able to do all of your analysis directly in Excel. However, if you're interviewing for data science or more technical analytics roles, you might need to use Tableau, SQL, or R to work with the data (for example, if it has millions of rows).

Once you complete your analysis, expect to make a five-to-ten-slide deck to communicate your insights and recommendations. Unless specified, you should be able to use any software or tools to do so. The most common ones are Google Slides and Microsoft PowerPoint.

When you finish your slides, you'll submit them to the interviewer. In the final round, you may be asked to present your slides and findings. During this presentation, your interviewer will probably ask follow-up questions regarding your work.

What Are Interviewers Looking For?

Your interviewers are trying to gauge your baseline level of analytics and slide making in order to see if you have what it takes to become a BizOps analyst. There are three qualities your interviewers are looking for: correct calculation and data analysis, appropriate insights and takeaways, and clear and concise communication on slides (written) and delivery of presentation (verbal). To elaborate more on the first point, your interviewers will want to make sure you have calculated your numbers correctly. They'll want to see that you pay attention to detail and sanity check your numbers.

Let's look at an example of someone approaching this in the wrong way.

During an interview I was conducting, I asked the candidate to break down the revenue equation for the Facebook feed into components and make assumptions for those component metrics.

Ideally, I was looking for this:

> Daily active users (DAU) × Facebook feed time/DAU (time spent/user) × ad impressions/Facebook feed time (ad load) × CPM (revenue/ad impressions × 1,000, also known as "cost per mille") = revenue

The interviewee had clearly memorized some of Facebook's key metrics, but they used them with this equation below and stated:

Daily active users × ad load = revenue

In this example, expanding the equation shows daily active users × ad impressions/Facebook feed time (ad load), which does not equal revenue, so this is clearly incorrect because the units don't cancel out. If, instead, he had said daily active users × revenue/user = revenue, that would have been a great starting point, and I would have just asked him to expand upon the latter metric. When you multiply through your metrics to get to the final answer, you should check that the final answer contains the correct units.

For the second point, your interviewers want to see that you can extract the right insights from the data. You should be able to identify key takeaways and come up with recommendations for the team.

I've seen candidates label slides with titles like "Ad Revenue by Country" or "Top Advertisers by Region." This summarizes the charts but doesn't synthesize the main takeaway for the audience. Instead, a slide title like "Ad Revenue is growing 40% YoY, driven by Feb launch of an incentive program for new advertisers" will lead the audience to the conclusion that you're trying to drive home.

For the third point, your interviewers want to see that you can communicate your recommendations succinctly and effectively. Make sure your slides are easy to follow and concisely cover the main takeaways. In the next few sections, I'll cover additional recommendations for creating these slides.

How to Complete the Take-Home Challenge in Eight Steps

Below are eight steps I use to complete a data challenge:

1. Understand the question.
2. Familiarize yourself with the data.
3. Clean the data.
4. Create a hypothesis.
5. Analyze the data.
6. Synthesize the data.
7. Create the slides.
8. Practice presenting the slides.

Now consider this take-home assignment example:

You have a dataset of Google's top advertisers globally. Each row in the dataset represents a different advertiser. The columns have metrics such as region, country, advertiser vertical, primary product, if they were offered a coupon, coupon cost, annual revenue, and advertiser satisfaction score. The objective of the challenge is to determine which advertisers the marketing team should target next with coupons.

Let's walk through each step, in detail, to make sure your submission will stand out from the crowd.

1. Understand the Question

The first and most important step to completing a take-home assignment is to understand what the question is asking. What's the objective of this analysis? Answering the wrong question—for example, one that you want to answer or one that is easier to answer—is the quickest way to fail a take-home challenge.

The best way to do this is to frequently refer back to the primary question when you're doing your analysis. If you find yourself going down rabbit holes that do not bring you closer to answering the question, stop exploring those: they are likely unimportant or not relevant. Pause and take a step back every so often to connect what you're doing back to the problem. Doing your due diligence to understand the question and what the interviewer really wants from you early on can save you hours of unnecessary work.

2. Familiarize Yourself with the Data

Once you understand the objective of the take-home challenge, familiarize yourself with the dataset. What do the rows and columns represent? This will help you gauge what types of analyses are possible.

Typically, each row in the dataset will represent a type of ID (user ID, customer ID, advertiser ID, email ID, etc.), and the columns will show different metrics. In the take-home assignment example, you would likely have a different advertiser (advertiser ID) in each row and then separate columns for metrics like region, product, coupon costs, annual revenue, and so on.

3. Clean the Data

Once you've familiarized yourself with the data, it's time to check the data quality.

1. Remove any duplicate entries (this is often called deduplication).
2. Fix any structural errors like typos and strange naming conventions. For example, if you see both "N/A" and "Not Applicable" appear, rename for consistency so they can be analyzed in the same category.
3. Filter unwanted outliers if you have a legitimate reason to believe that there is an improper data entry.
4. Handle missing data using your judgment. Here are three options:
    a. Remove the row or column that has missing values. Doing so will drop or lose information, so be mindful of this decrease in sample size.
    b. Input missing values based on other data points. This could reduce accuracy, as you'll be using assumptions and not real observations.
    c. Leave it as is. This is the easiest route but could skew the results of your analysis.

4. Create a Hypothesis

Before even starting your data analysis, another helpful but often overlooked step that can keep you on track is generating an early hypothesis. An example of what a hypothesis would look like for our take-home example could be "Retail advertisers perform really well when their primary product is Google's Smart Shopping, so we should give retail customers a targeted coupon to adopt this product if they don't use it already." This step helps anchor you on what data you would need to either prove or disprove your hypothesis, and it will help you focus on answering the question.

Next, think about three to five broad areas that would be most important to help you prove or disprove your hypothesis. Defining these up front can focus the analyses needed to solve the problem and identify the most relevant data you'll want to pull to support your claim. If your three to five broader areas are MECE, that's even better. MECE stands for "mutually exclusive, collectively exhaustive" and means that the "buckets" you're analyzing do not overlap and that they cover the entire scope of what you're looking at. An example of three MECE buckets for the retail customers hypothesis might be "existing customers," "churned customers," and "new customers." Within each of these buckets, you can determine if the data shows that a coupon is the right answer for these populations. Defining the story up front can focus the analysis needed to solve the problem.

5. Analyze the Data

Now that you have your framework, you can dive into the data analysis portion. Analytics requires critical thinking to look for the why behind your data and use metrics to guide decision-making. The first step is to identify basic metrics you want to analyze. See how these metrics in the dataset vary across different groups and make note of any variations you see.

In terms of this example challenge, a basic metric you could analyze is how annual revenue differs across advertisers that weren't offered a coupon. You could propose that Google focuses on providing incentives to advertisers that have the highest annual revenue, in order to reward and sustain these types of customers.

The second type of analysis you could do involves making compound metrics (metrics that are derived from two or more metrics). In order to do this, you'd create a new column or row in Excel to compute the metric.

In terms of the Google example, a compound metric you could analyze is ROI = revenue / costs. For the current advertisers with a coupon, you can see what the sum(annual revenue)/sum(coupon cost) looks like by different regions, countries, verticals, and products. Then, you could identify a certain persona that would be a perfect target audience for the coupon.

Many business decisions require looking at the total opportunity from a revenue and cost perspective, so it's best to include compound metrics like ROI in an analysis for a more holistic picture.

The third type of analysis is forecast modeling. Based on certain assumptions and existing data, you can create a model to make a prediction or forecast.

Let's say you've identified a list of two hundred advertisers in the e-commerce vertical (top revenue advertisers in the highest ROI-generating vertical) that Google's marketing team should target next with coupons. You could use the data on the current e-commerce advertisers without coupons and make assumptions on how much improvement is possible through the coupon incentive. You could then create a model to predict how much annual revenues will increase.

Given that most of these take-home challenges are in Excel, I thought I would share the most useful Excel functions I use for these types of challenges (listed below). These are also the same functions I use for my day-to-day work. I've included a quick description of each one, but I encourage you to look them up and practice them if they're not familiar.

VLOOKUP: VLOOKUP is a formula that allows you to link data from two different sources based on a unique key.

Pivot Table: Pivot tables allow you to slice and dice the data along any dimension you want, which very quickly gives you an idea of what the data looks like and where you'll need to dig deeper.

MATCH: MATCH returns either the row number or column number of a value you're looking for in a table.

INDEX: INDEX is basically a VLOOKUP on steroids, and the best part of the index formula is that the lookup value doesn't need to be in the first column of the lookup table.

SUMIFS: The SUMIFS formula allows you to return the sum of a specified column based on certain conditions.

COUNTIFS: Similar to the SUMIFS formula above, COUNTIFS allows you to quickly summarize data using basically the same syntax.

IFERROR: This is a nifty function to clean up your model output from errors and replace with a custom value of your choice. There is a specific IFNA function with the same syntax to specifically catch and replace #N/A errors.

&: If you want to combine two cells, you can do that quickly with Cell1&Cell2.

YEAR(), MONTH(), and DAY(): Dates are tricky

because every data source seems to represent them differently. You can use Excel to convert dates to the same format across sources.

VALUE(): This converts a text field to numbers.

TEXT(): This converts numbers to text.

LEFT, RIGHT, and MID: These functions help you select pieces of text that you need.

6. Synthesize the Data

Once you've completed your analysis, you'll need to decide on an answer or recommendation. Throughout your analysis, you should be writing down key takeaways for every metric. Skim through these takeaways and decide on what answer they collectively support. Does it prove or disprove your hypothesis? It may not be black and white—often, you'll have some key takeaways that support your hypothesis and others that disprove it. You'll need to take time to review conflicting insights and decide what's most important. Regardless of what you end up deciding, you should address the opposing insights.

In the example, let's say your data analysis showed that the majority of Google's customers are retail customers, and existing retail customers that use Google's Smart Shopping product perform three times better in annual revenue than those that don't. This is great because this supports your hypothesis that Google should target retail customers with a coupon to incentivize them to adopt this product. However, another cut of the data shows that this retail population with Smart Shopping has the lowest customer satisfaction score. What should you do when the two conclusions oppose each other in this way?

In this case, I recommend doing a deep dive into the data first and understanding the low customer satisfaction scores better. For example, it could be that these retail advertisers using Smart Shopping are unhappy about how long it takes to see returns on their end, but once they do see returns, they spend a lot on the product. Once you identify whether or not this low customer satisfaction score is fixable, then you can go forward with your recommendation: the marketing team should target coupons toward retail customers that are missing Smart Shopping and include a stipulation that they must adopt the Smart Shopping product in order to get the coupon.

Addressing the opposing insights will ensure that you've conducted a thorough analysis and will make your recommendation even more credible.

Last, think about what additional data or qualitative insights would be helpful to strengthen your argument. Include these as next steps to let the interviewers know that you've thought about every angle of the prompt at hand.

7. Create the Slides

The point of the slides is to showcase your work and recommendations and ultimately drive a business decision. Even if you do outstanding data analysis, the interviewer won't be able to tell if you can't make great slides.

Your slides will need to tell a story that is clear, concise, easy to understand, and backed by data. Here's the structure I use when making my presentation slides:

1. Title slide
2. Executive summary
3. Supporting analysis
4. Risks and mitigations

5. Conclusion and next steps
6. Appendix

Let's go through each in turn and look at how they should be presented.

Title slide: The title slide should be simple and include your presentation title and name. If you'd like, you can also include the logo of the company you're interviewing with.

Executive summary: The executive summary is probably the easiest part to put together. If you've synthesized the data and made your action-based headlines correctly on the rest of the presentation, you'll just need to take these (which should already be in bold so they're easy to see) and place them in order here. The reader should be able to understand your story by just reading this slide alone. If, after creating the executive summary, you find that the story doesn't flow as well as you'd hoped, you may need to rethink your storyline or your action-based headlines to fix this problem.

Supporting analysis: These slides should make up the majority of your presentation. Here you'll include charts, graphs, tables, and bullet points that support your answer or recommendation.

Write one-sentence action-based headlines for each of these slides in the presentation. Make sure you synthesize: create an insight with recommendations that can be acted upon. As mentioned in previous chapters, there's a major difference between a summary and a synthesis. A summary is a restatement of facts. Synthesis means digesting those facts and developing an insight into what the client should do and why they should do it.

Risks and mitigations: Include a slide that lists the major risks of your recommendation (e.g., assumptions that could be questioned). By addressing these risks and listing out actions to mitigate them, your recommendation will be much stronger.

Conclusion and next steps: Reiterate your answer and recommendations in this slide. Include a list of next steps outlining what you'd do with more data or more time. Consider the following questions to help you brainstorm ideas:

- Is there any more data you would want to collect to provide stronger support for your answer?
- If you weren't as time constrained, what other analyses would you explore?
- What stakeholders would you need to secure buy-in from in order to execute the recommendation or decision?

Appendix: Feel free to include backup slides in the appendix section. These could be analyses you've explored that don't fit in with the main storyline. These slides can also show assumptions or backup calculations.

One example of an appendix slide is a sensitivity analysis. This considers "what ifs" to show what the change in the result would look like under different assumptions. For example, if you had assumed coupon revenue incrementality to be 10 percent in your main analysis, you can show what the end results would have looked like if you had assumed 5 percent or 15 percent instead. This type of analysis can increase your confidence that your conclusion will hold under a range of assumptions.

8. Practice Presenting the Slides

Communicating and presenting your slides is how your work "shows up." It can make all the difference between a great and a not-so-great outcome from your analysis.

Focusing on what matters means focusing on your audience, and the way you present your slides will depend greatly on whom you're presenting to. Some examples of different stakeholders follow, and I've listed the questions that they may ask (or think about) when you are presenting so you can think about what their priorities and perspective might be. You should try to step into their shoes to consider, "So what? Why should I care?"

Marketing Executives

- Is this going to make Google more money?
- Does it inform a decision I need to make?
- Does it support any other strategic initiative?
- Where will the budget come from? How much funding do we need for these coupons? What could we be funding instead?

Marketing Managers

- Does this coupon initiative help the performance of my team?

- Does it help me reach my revenue targets?
- How can I use this analysis?

Sellers

- Does this coupon initiative help me individually?
- How can I use this analysis?

Stories versus Reports

The mistake most people make when presenting data analysis is thinking too much about the data. They want to capture everything as fully and accurately as possible, but they fail to consider the importance of conveying the key message in a way that will stimulate action. But what does this mean in practice?

Since the audience will likely not have been in the weeds of the data analysis as you have, try to keep it more high-level and client friendly. Avoid including dense or detailed information. Avoid large tables of numbers. State your findings, actions, and recommendations in a way that your audience can understand easily and that is convincing. If people are not persuaded, nothing will happen. The answer is in telling a story.

Stories answer the question "Why is this important?" A story is a logical progression of thought, interprets the data and makes a judgment, has a conclusion and a main point, and only shows data that is relevant to the main point.

Stories are easy to spot compared to reports. Which one of these executive summaries is a story and which is a report?

Executive Summary Example One

Google's agency revenue has increased by 40%. However, non-agency revenue has decreased by 20%.

Non-agency revenue decreased primarily due to

- strategic change in marketing lead generation.
- change in advertiser purchasing preferences.

Google can reverse the trend in non-agency revenue by

- changing the mix of marketing campaign spend.
- launching a new training program to teach new advertising trends.

Executive Summary Example Two

Google's agency versus non-agency revenue:

- Agency +40%
- Non-agency +20%

Google's YoY revenue by region:

- Americas +15%
- APAC +20%
- EMEA +18%

Marketing communications events:

- Creative campaign
- Phone number changes
- Sign in remodel

Google's YoY headcount:

- Increased +20%
- Revenue per headcount +5%

Example two is just a bunch of data points. There is not a single conclusion that the readers will come to by reading this executive summary. Meanwhile, example one interprets the data and gives suggestions on what the team should do to reverse the trend. We should all aim to create executive summaries like that in example one.

Tips for Slide Formatting

Here are several tips for formatting your slides to ensure the information is presented clearly and persuasively.

When you're creating your slides, use a variety of formats to keep the audience engaged. Below are some essential slide formats for each part of your presentation that can help you drive your point home:

Executive summary slide

Topic 1

1. Supporting point 1
2. Supporting point 2
3. Supporting point 3

Topic 2

4. Supporting point 4
5. Supporting point 5

Topic 3

6. Supporting point 6
7. Supporting point 7

Framing slide option 1

Topic 1	Topic 2	Topic 3
• ...	• ...	• ...

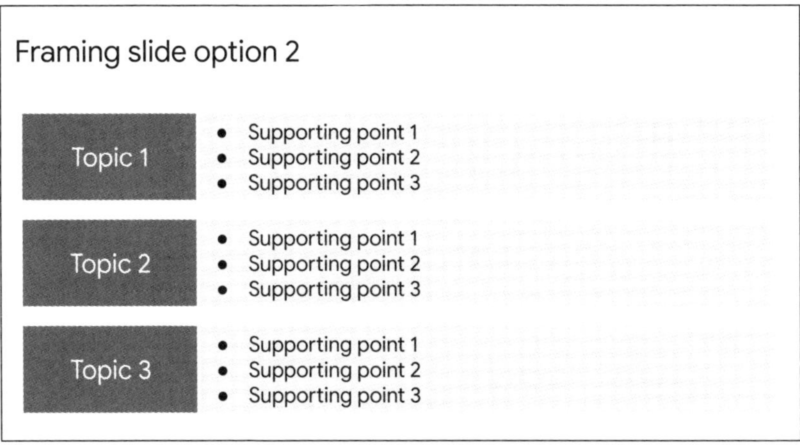

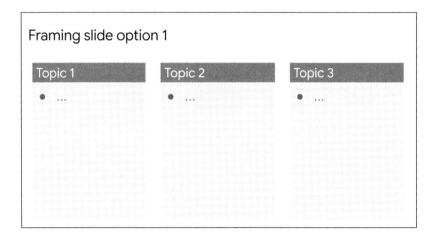

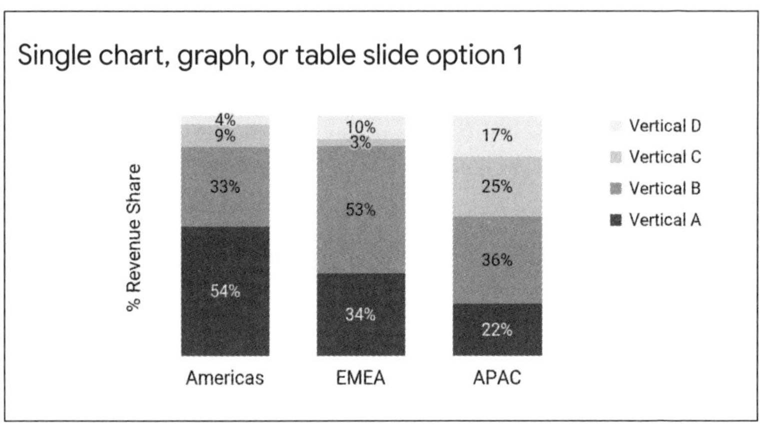

Single chart, graph, or table slide option 2

	Option 1	**Option 2**
Metric 1	x%	y%
Metric 2	x%	y%
Metric 3	x%	y%
Metric 4	x%	y%
Metric 5	x%	y%
Metric 6	x%	y%

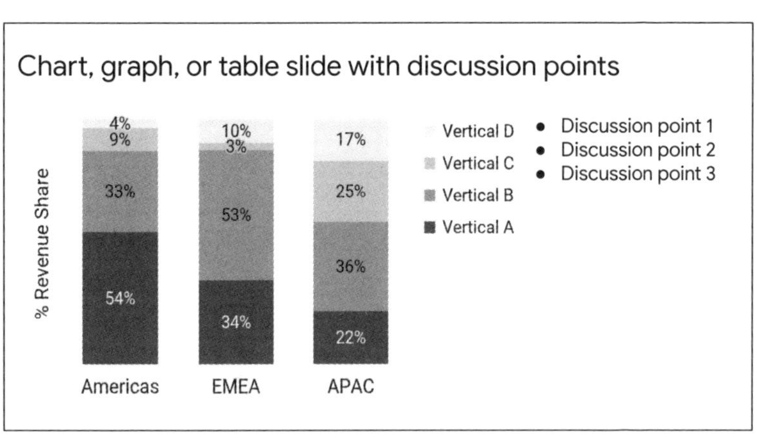

Once you've gotten a handle on creating the slide formats, focus on making each slide easier to read and digest. You can accomplish this by doing the following to draw the audience's attention to the most important points:

Use a slide tracker to visually show where the audience is on your roadmap.

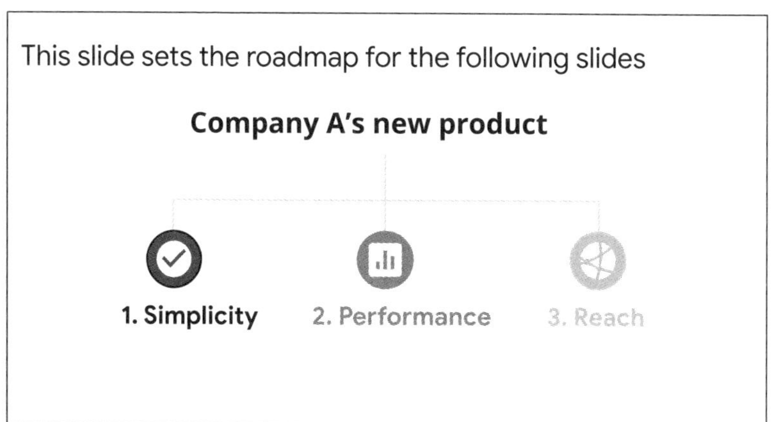
This slide sets the roadmap for the following slides
Company A's new product
1. Simplicity
2. Performance
3. Reach

1 | Simplicity

Slide trackers make it easier for the audience to follow

- This slide covers the first area: **simplicity.**
- The slide tracker on the **top left corner** indicates this.
- Make the slide tracker the **same color** as what's on the roadmap slide.

2 | Performance

Slide trackers make it easier for the audience to follow

- This slide covers the second area: **performance.**
- The slide tracker on the **top left corner** indicates this.
- Make the slide tracker the **same color** as what's on the roadmap slide.

3 | Reach

Slide trackers make it easier for the audience to follow

- This slide covers the third area: **reach.**
- The slide tracker on the **top left corner** indicates this.
- Make the slide tracker the **same color** as what's on the roadmap slide.

If a deck is longer than eight slides, slide trackers help the audience know where they are in the presentation and what topic to focus on. Otherwise, they may not be needed.

Circle or box the most important takeaway so that it stands out.

Circle/box important information to draw attention to that area

	Option 1	Option 2
YoY Revenue % Increase	22%	20%
Revenue	$8,000	$10,000
ROI	3.5	5.0

Bold the main points to ensure they are read and are memorable.

Bolding selectively can highlight certain points

- Make sure to **use bolding to draw attention** to the most important points.
- Examples are numbers like **$10M** or **45%**.
- **Do not overuse bolding**, or else it will lose its effect.
- Feel free to bold in a **different color** for additional emphasis.

Have a tagline or callout box at the bottom to highlight key takeaways.

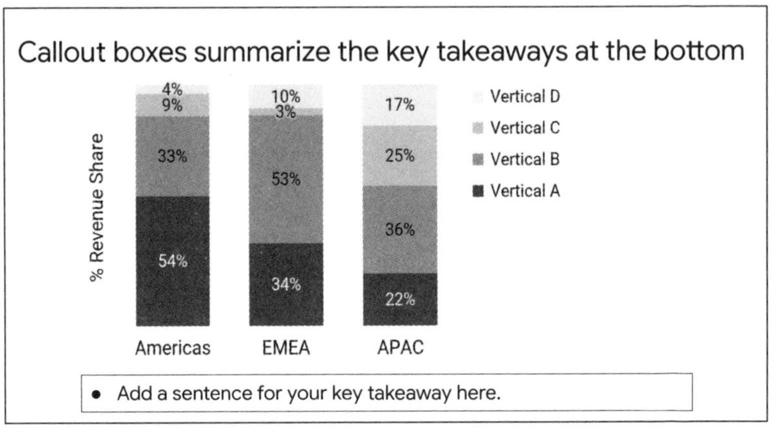

Use icons as visuals to make the presentation unique and memorable.

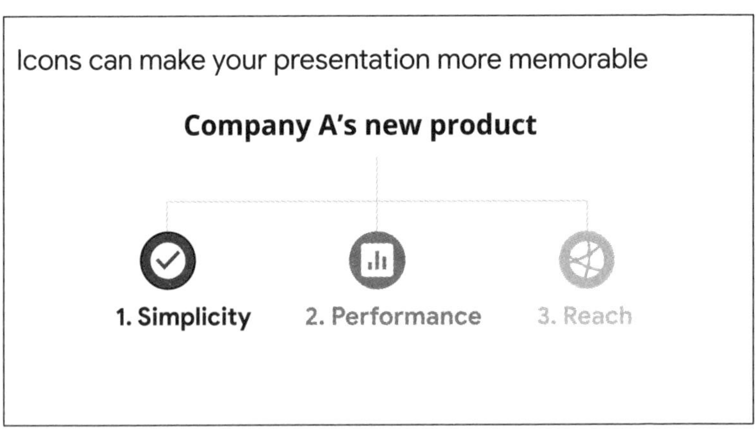

Keep in mind that audiences will tend to read your slide in the following order, so prioritize information accordingly.

And save this one for last

You will read this first

And then read this second

then this one

An Example of a Take-Home Challenge Solution

Let's walk through an example take-home challenge dataset and a potential solution with example slides. Note that the data I used in these charts is fabricated and does not reflect Google's actual performance or their actual interview questions.

Prompt

Based on the given dataset, what are the five insights or recommendations you'd share with the team for their next weekly business review meeting?

Data

The dataset contains the following information for small- and medium-sized businesses (SMBs):

> **Advertiser ID:** Each row is a unique advertiser identification number.
>
> **Advertiser type:** New versus existing customers. New customers are defined as ones that started advertising less

than one year ago. Meanwhile, existing customers have been with Google for more than a year.

Activation date: This is the date that the advertiser first started spending.

Advertiser vertical: This indicates which industry the advertiser's business is in. There are six industries in this dataset: retail, media and entertainment, healthcare, tech, travel, and finance.

Advertiser region: This indicates which region (Americas, EMEA, or APAC) that the advertiser was acquired in.

Revenue: This is the amount the advertiser paid Google over the past year.

Advertiser week 26 active flag: This is a binary 0 or 1 flag that indicates if the account was active 26 weeks after activation.

Google

Take-Home Challenge

Amy Sun Yan

Executive Summary

- A surge of new SMBs started during COVID-19, as entrepreneurs are starting businesses at the fastest rate in more than a decade.
- Key verticals are capturing new demand surge and move to digital: retail, media, and tech.
- Although there are many new advertisers, existing advertisers are more valuable than new advertisers across all industries.
- There's an especially strong recovery in the APAC region compared to the rest of the world.
    - Next step: Work with sales to understand underlying drivers and take learnings to other regions.

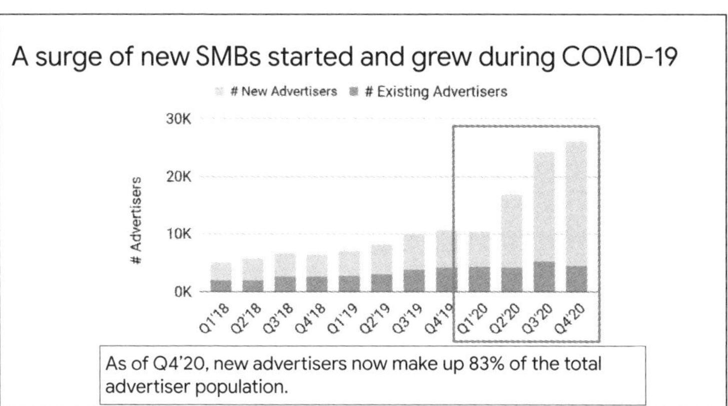

Key verticals are capturing new demand surge and move to digital: retail, media, and tech

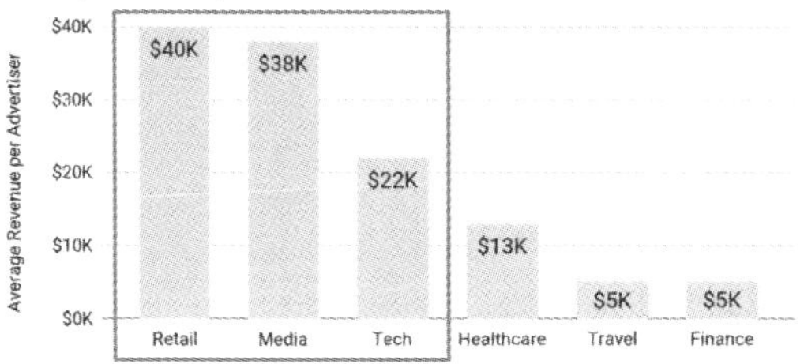

Average annual revenue from retail advertisers has grown to $40K, followed by media ($38K) and tech ($22K).

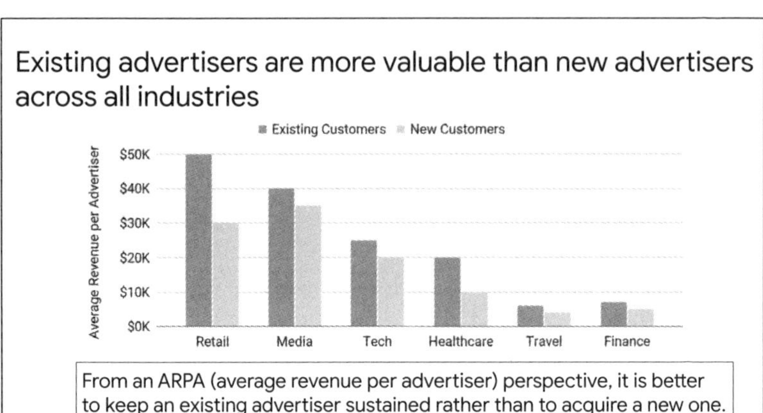
Existing advertisers are more valuable than new advertisers across all industries
Existing Customers
New Customers
Average Revenue per Advertiser
$50K
$40K
$30K
$20K
$10K
$0K
Retail
Media
Tech
Healthcare
Travel
Finance
From an ARPA (average revenue per advertiser) perspective, it is better to keep an existing advertiser sustained rather than to acquire a new one.

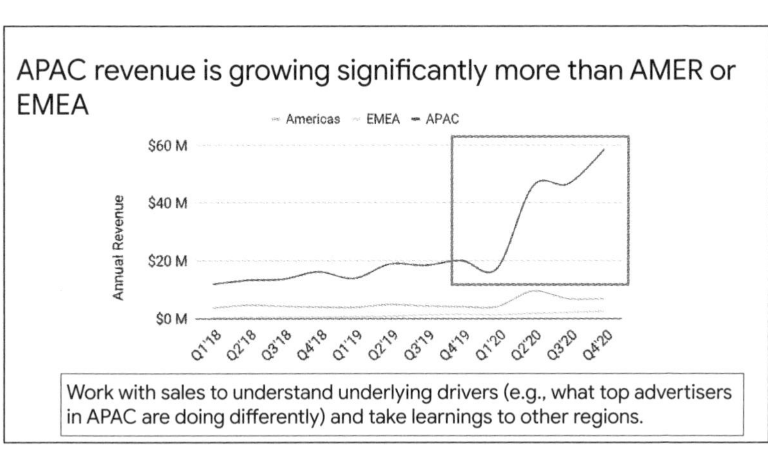
APAC revenue is growing significantly more than AMER or EMEA
Americas
EMEA
APAC
Annual Revenue
$60 M
$40 M
$20 M
$0 M
Q1'18
Q2'18
Q3'18
Q4'18
Q1'19
Q2'19
Q3'19
Q4'19
Q1'20
Q2'20
Q3'20
Q4'20
Work with sales to understand underlying drivers (e.g., what top advertisers in APAC are doing differently) and take learnings to other regions.

PART THREE

Landing the Job in BizOps

13

The Art of Following Up

I REMEMBER THE STRUGGLE of applying for a lot of jobs and trying to make connections with the right people after graduating. One important lesson I learned early on was to follow up with recruiters, employees, and hiring managers after our conversations. For example, the Google recruiter I initially talked to about a contractor position (which I rejected) ended up reaching back out to me a few months later for a full-time role (my current job!). Just by maintaining good relationships and keeping in touch through emails, I was able to secure a full-time role at Google without even having applied for it.

In a similar vein, with Facebook, I had applied and gotten rejected from the Oculus BizOps role after my on-site interview. I was devastated when I got the rejection email and thought the recruiter was just being polite when they asked to "stay in touch." Luckily, I did keep in touch, and that same recruiter ended up sharing the Facebook Newsfeed BizOps role that I interviewed and got the offer for (more than a year after my initial contact with the recruiter). Hopefully my real-life examples illustrate how important it is to follow up!

I've collaborated with Oliver Pour (former Program Manager Intern at Amazon) on this chapter. Our guide utilizes hard-won lessons from our own life experiences to create a resource bank. It covers several situations in job hunting when you should follow up, such as when you've met someone at a career fair or when you've finished an interview, and provides suggestions of how to do it effectively and professionally. In each scenario, we dive into the key things to include in a message and a real-life example for each.

When You Make Contact via LinkedIn

Let's say you've been browsing LinkedIn and found someone who has your dream job and position, so you've invited them to connect. Great, now they've accepted! It's crucial that you follow this up with an invitation to chat and get to know them better. Just think about it this way: sending a connection request to someone and then just ignoring each other is the same as meeting someone and then never seeing them again in your life. If you don't reach out, these people will forget about you. First impressions matter a lot, so your follow-ups are of immense importance to create a strong connection!

Below is a template and example to help get you started.

Key Things to Include

- Buffer line of greeting
- Introduction: name, year/university
- Why are you reaching out?
- Encourage them to keep in touch.

Example

> Hi Amy,
>
> Thanks for connecting with me, and I hope you're well! My name is Oliver Pour, a current sophomore at Boston University. I wanted to reach out to see if you are available

to speak sometime. I would love to learn about your experiences at Meta. Looking forward to hearing from you!

Thank you,

Oliver

When They Ask You to Circle Back Another Time

A common phrase used in the office is "circle back," which means that someone wants to discuss something at a later time. If you've reached out to somebody and their calendar is booked for the next few weeks, they might ask you to circle back and reach out another time. You'll want to respect their space and then send a reminder once they're ready to talk.

Key Things to Include

- Reply to the previous message where they asked to circle back to give context.
- What is your ask?
    - » An introduction to . . .
    - » Resume review
    - » LinkedIn profile review
    - » General questions about the role or company
- When are you available to speak?

Example

Hi Anna,

I hope all is well! I wanted to follow up in hopes that you

would have fifteen minutes to speak. I would love to learn about your role at Spotify and hear more about your experiences as a member of the business operations team. I am available next Monday and Tuesday from 12:00 to 4:00 p.m. Please let me know if you are free. If not, I would be happy to accommodate your schedule.

Thank you in advance,

Jenny

When You've Had No Response to Your Prior Email

If you haven't gotten a response after an initial meeting request, it's possible your email got lost in the recipient's inbox or they simply forgot to respond. In situations like these, a quick reminder message may be all they need to get back to you.

Key Things to Include

- Restate the context of the original email.
- Include a clear ask:
  - » An introduction to . . .
  - » Resume review
  - » LinkedIn profile review
  - » General questions about the role or company
- Flag any additional resources for them to review:
  - » LinkedIn profile
  - » Resume

Example

Hi Priya,

I hope all is well. I just wanted to follow up on the message I sent last Thursday about a possible call in the near future. I am actually considering operations as a career, and I was wondering if you might be able to provide any insight on your experience at Reddit or let me know who would? Any feedback would be helpful!

I attached my resume for you to take a look at to learn more about me if you would like! If you have fifteen minutes to talk in the upcoming couple of days, I would love to speak more to you over a phone call. My availability for this week consists of Thursday and Friday after 1:00 p.m. PDT. Do any of those times work for your schedule? Please let me know!

Thank you,

Dmitriy

When You've Had a Meetup

After a career fair or other type of event, sending a follow-up email is a great way to remind the person who you are and allow you to clarify your request, if you have one. For example, maybe you're looking to schedule a meeting with someone you met to continue building your relationship with them. You can request that phone call or meeting in your message.

Key Things to Include

- How did you meet?

- What was one takeaway you had from your conversation?
- What is your ask?
    - » Phone call
    - » Resume review
    - » LinkedIn profile review
    - » General questions about the role or company

Example

Hi Kristina,

It was great meeting you at the Boston University Career Fair last week. I loved hearing about your involvement with the Boston University Student Government in 2016; it was truly a pleasure. I'm really interested to learn more about your current role in the product strategy team at Salesforce, as a career in strategy is something I would like to pursue in the future. If you have fifteen minutes to talk in the upcoming couple of days, I would love to speak more to you over a phone call. My availability for this week consists of Monday, Tuesday, and Wednesday mornings between 8:00 and 11:00 a.m. EST. Do any of those times work for your schedule? Please let me know!

Thank you in advance,

Maria

When You've Had a Phone Call

After someone has taken time out of their day to chat with you, it's important to send a follow-up thank-you message! This message is there to build and strengthen the relationship for the future. In this follow-up message, describe concrete results your contact helped you achieve and express why that result is meaningful.

Another rule is to pay it forward when possible. In return for their help, you can provide something valuable to this person in the form of an introduction or a relevant resource that demonstrates your gratitude and the fact that you're not just looking for a one-way relationship.

Key Things to Include

- Thanks and appreciation
- What is one takeaway you had from your conversation?
- What is one thing you enjoyed about the conversation?
- Pay it forward:
    - » Share an introduction.
    - » Share a relevant resource.
- What is your ask?
    - » An introduction to . . .
    - » Resume review
    - » LinkedIn profile review
    - » General questions about the role or company
- Encourage them to keep in touch.

Example

Hi Aubrey,

I wanted to thank you for the phone call on April 29. It was a pleasure meeting you and learning about your experiences at NVIDIA. One main takeaway I had from our conversation was to always reach out to the recruiter of a role you would like to apply for to learn more. I enjoyed hearing about your new puppy Luna and all the adventures you've had so far.

I also remember you mentioned that you'd love to speak with someone in the chief of staff role to pick their brain—I've just started a chat thread between you and my friend Ali who is currently chief of staff at Stripe.

I would greatly appreciate it if you could give me feedback on my LinkedIn profile whenever you have the chance. Once again, thank you for taking the time out of your busy schedule to speak with me. I hope we keep in touch!

All the best,

Evan

When You Want to Check In after a Period of Time

Now that you've had one or several conversations with this person, it's important to maintain the relationship by checking in after a period of time (I'd recommend every six months). The best time to check in is when you've felt the impact of their guidance (e.g., you landed a job offer by following their suggestions).

Key Things to Include

- Reference the last time you spoke for context.
- Thanks and appreciation
- Highlight one piece of advice they gave you.
- Explain the impact their advice had.
- Encourage them to keep in touch.

Example

> Hi Jesse,
>
> I hope you are doing well. I just wanted to check in and say hello! It was a pleasure speaking with you in early April and I appreciate you taking the time out of your busy schedule to tell me about your experiences at Apple. I took your advice on sending LinkedIn messages to professionals that have posted about internships, and it has helped me in several ways, such as earning an interview for a strategy and operations role at a dream company of mine.
>
> Once again, thank you for all of your guidance. I look forward to speaking again in the near future!
>
> Best,
>
> Haylie

When You've Had an Interview

Let's assume that you had the amazing opportunity to interview at your dream company! Your next step should be to send a thank-you note to each of the interviewers within two days of the interview. Only one in twenty candidates does this, so doing this small act will make you a stand-out, superstar candidate.[26]

By writing a thoughtful follow-up expressing your enthusiasm for the job, thanking them for their time, and including anecdotes from the conversation, you'll also be demonstrating strong soft skills and thus making yourself more memorable as a candidate. These skills, like communication and active listening, are highly sought after.

Key Things to Include

- Thanks and appreciation
- What is one thing you enjoyed about the conversation?
- Explain why you think you'd be successful in this role.
- Encourage them to keep in touch.

Example

> Hi Darren,
>
> Thank you for taking the time to speak with me last Friday about the business operations role at Amazon. It was a pleasure talking with you, and I really enjoyed hearing all the details you shared about the opportunity.
>
> As someone who also likes seeing the tangible results of my work, I enjoyed hearing you talk about A/B testing within your role and how it allows you to see the outcome fairly quickly. I am confident that my skills will allow me

26 Margaret Buj, "When and How to Follow Up after an Interview," LiveCareer, accessed May 22, 2021, https://www.livecareer.com/resources/interviews/prep/job-interview-follow-up.

to come in and succeed in this role, and it's a position I'd be excited to take on.

I'm looking forward to hearing from you about the next steps, and please don't hesitate to contact me in the meantime if you have any questions!

Thank you,

Sage

When You're Accepting a Job Offer

You've put in the hard work and now you've got the offer—congratulations! It's standard practice to send an acceptance email to officially accept the job offer. This will help you get your new job off to a professional start and allow you to express your gratitude for the opportunity.

Key Things to Include

- Give thanks and appreciation.
- Formally accept the job offer.
- Clarify your start date.
- Ask if anything else is needed.
- If you haven't already, clarify your terms and conditions for employment to prevent future misunderstanding (i.e., salary, benefits, work schedule, etc.).

Example

Hi Rohan,

As we discussed on the phone, I'm very pleased to accept the position of business operations analyst with Epic Games and look forward to starting this role on July 1. Thank you again for this opportunity, and I'm excited to work with John and his team.

If there's any additional information or paperwork you need prior to my start date, please let me know.

Thank you,

Stephanie

When You're Declining a Job Offer

Before sending a declination of an offer letter, make sure you're positive you do not want the job. If a scenario exists where you'd take the job if there were a pay increase, first try to negotiate a counter offer (refer to chapter 14).

If you've considered the opportunity well and have decided not to accept it, sending a polite, grateful, and timely rejection letter is a fantastic way to maintain a good relationship with the employer. You never know when your paths may cross again.

Key Things to Include

- Give thanks and appreciation.
- Give a good, brief reason for declining.
- Ask to stay in touch.

Example

Hi Muhammad,

Thank you very much for offering me the position of business operations analyst at Snapchat. It was a difficult decision to make but, unfortunately, I cannot accept your offer at this time, as I've already signed an offer with another company.

I sincerely appreciate you taking the time to interview me and sharing information about the opportunity and company. Again, thank you for your consideration. I hope we can keep in touch in case future opportunities arise.

Thanks,

Helen

14

Salary Negotiation

YOU'VE BEEN OFFERED THE job! Now comes the critical discussion around salary. It's likely that you'll know the pay band within which the position sits, but you will need to negotiate the final base salary as well as other benefits, such as a signing bonus or equity.

Salary negotiation can be a tricky area to navigate, and it's often not talked about openly. This air of mystery puts you on the back foot and makes it harder to develop a clear strategy that will lead to the best result. It may feel jarring to suddenly be making demands of the company that you wanted to hire you, but it's important that you keep your long-term needs in mind. Your salary is not only what will pay your bills, it is what will flag your worth at that point in your career and provide a foundation for growth.

Some of my mentees have been uncomfortable asking for more because they're afraid that the recruiter will get mad and rescind the offer. However, I'm here to tell you that your job offer is *not* going to be taken away from you as long as you've negotiated respectfully and have been truthful throughout the interview process. The worst-case scenario is that they politely say no and remain firm on the initial offer numbers. Remember: nothing ventured, nothing gained!

In this chapter, I'll cover useful tips for negotiation as well as a breakdown of components of salary, how to research and benchmark, and other benefits to consider.

Tips for Salary Negotiation

Google added an extra $15,000 to my signing bonus when I was negotiating for my current role, and all it took was a ten-minute call with my recruiter. Friends at companies like Meta, Amazon, and DoorDash managed to negotiate even more significant pay increases, often in just one or two quick calls. That's why I believe these tips for salary negotiation are so important and one of the highest ROI skills you can make time to learn.

In reality, most people don't spend time on this and come woefully unprepared. They try to wing it and inevitably stumble, leaving money behind on the negotiation table. This isn't surprising because recruiters negotiate for a living. You don't.

So, in order to level the playing field, I thought it would be helpful to share some ground rules that I've learned over time that will make salary negotiation that little bit easier.

Be Polite and Likeable, but Don't "Suck Up"

Your recruiter is your advocate, and they will be pushing for your success if they like you, so make sure that you nurture this relationship. However, it's best that you do this in an authentic and natural way by being yourself rather than trying to manipulate the situation to your advantage, as you may come across as fake. My Google recruiter ended up going back four different times to the compensation committee to get higher numbers for me. I ended up sharing baking recipes with my recruiter since we connected on that hobby!

Justify Your Demands

Remember to explain *why* you require what you're asking for. Help them to understand why you deserve it.

For instance, if my new base salary was slightly lower than my old base (but all other compensation was higher), I'd still ask for some kind of replacement compensation in the form of stocks or a signing bonus as parity with a previous role, which is a reasonable expectation.

When I was moving from Facebook (before it became Meta) to Google, I was giving up a few referral bonuses I was supposed to get at Facebook soon. I let Google know, and they compensated me accordingly so I wouldn't feel like I was missing out by moving companies.

If you're moving cities, make sure you do your research on what the cost-of-living differences should be (you can use NerdWallet's Cost of Living Calculator online).[27] This type of research can help you stay firm on your salary request, as this has a tangible impact on your expenses and can change the real-world value of your pay. You could get an additional $5,000 to $10,000 during the negotiation process through this technique.

In my experience, Facebook and Google will move on base salary, but not very much. They're usually more flexible when you have not disclosed salary history or expectations. That doesn't mean you shouldn't ask for more base salary, but it does mean that specific request may result in a smaller increase. It is worth considering other, more aggressive moves that are not related to base salary, such as asking for more equity.

Don't Reveal Your Current Salary

Your recruiter will ask for your salary history, or at least your current salary, if it's legal in their state.

Do not tell them your current salary. If you do, the base salary component of your job offer will probably only be slightly above your current salary, and it will be challenging to negotiate a substantial increase once they make your job offer.

---

27 "NerdWallet's Cost of Living Calculator," NerdWallet, accessed July 12, 2020, https://www.nerdwallet.com/cost-of-living-calculator.

They will usually also ask for your salary expectations. That request will sound something like this: "So, what were you hoping for in terms of compensation if you come aboard here at Google?"

Do not tell them your salary expectations. While they might have a good idea of the value of that job to Google's business, you would only be guessing what they might pay someone with your skillset and experience. You will practically always guess wrong and cost yourself money later on.

If you do guess, the company will hold on tight to these numbers, and it can be very, very challenging to get them to move once they know that is what you are aiming for. So, avoid sharing that information if at all possible.[28]

While you want the recruiter to say the first number (so you don't anchor too low), it's important to have a range ready to go in case you are pushed. I like to say something along the lines of this: "While I'm still interested in understanding more about the role, based on my research I believe the market rate for this position is between X and Y." Make sure you're prepared to accept close to the lower end of your stated range.

If you do get ahold of salary information from current employees in the role you're interested in, you could then respond with your salary expectations and range based on a more educated guess. However, you should always start higher than what you think you could realistically get. The company will find some way to compensate you if they figure you're worth it.

Make It Clear That They Can Get You

Accepting a job offer is a balancing act. You don't want to let them know that you're desperate to work for them and be offered a lower salary than you deserve. But recruiters are also not willing to spend

28 Josh Doody, "Got a Job Offer from Google? Here's How to Negotiate It!" Fearless Salary Negotiation, accessed July 13, 2020, https://fearlesssalary negotiation.com/google-salary-negotiation/.

time and effort on you if you're likely to say "no, thank you" at the end of the recruiting process. Even if you take a strong position on your salary expectations, make it clear that you're serious about working for this employer. Meanwhile, you should also make sure to mention any other job options that you have as leverage and then balance that out by saying why—or under what conditions—you would be happy to forgo those options and accept the offer.

Understand the Constraints

Even if they like you and want to give you what you want, they may have certain hard constraints, such as salary caps for the level you interviewed for, that no amount of negotiation can loosen. Your job is to figure out where they're flexible and where they're not so you can negotiate effectively.

I like to start with raising the base salary as much as possible and then focusing on each component of the package until the recruiter says there's no room left to budge. Some companies may be flexible on start dates, vacation time, or signing bonuses. Other companies might allow you to negotiate the initial salary offer or job title. The better you understand the constraints, the more likely you'll be able to propose an option that will satisfy both parties!

Consider Everything Holistically

It's not just about the money. Much of your satisfaction from a job will come from other factors you can negotiate, perhaps even more easily than salary. Focus on the entire deal: your responsibilities, travel, location, flexibility of work hours, opportunities for promotion and growth, office perks, support for continued education, and so on. Last, think about the long term. You may chart out a course that pays less handsomely now but will put you in a stronger position later down the road. For example, if you're currently a level four BizOps analyst and you've decided that you want to pivot to a product manager role, it's okay to take a lower level (level three) associate product manager role in order to get on the track you're more interested in.

Think About Timing of Offers to Maximize Opportunity

When you're starting to job hunt, you often want to get at least one offer to feel secure. Getting multiple offers helps with negotiation because you have a greater ability to walk away if the negotiation doesn't work out in your favor. This is especially true for those finishing a degree program, when everyone is interviewing and many are celebrating early victories. Ironically, an early offer can be problematic: once a company makes an offer, it will expect an answer reasonably soon (often in one to two weeks). If you decide to take it, you will then forgo any other opportunities that might be on the horizon. If you decide to decline it, you will return to that precarious position of being without an offer on the table. To give yourself the best chance of securing a good salary in the right role, it's more useful to have all of your offers arrive close together to make negotiation easier. You can then compare and contrast and use them as leverage. One subtle way to solve this problem is to delay a round of interviews, and ask for a later second- or third-round interview. I was traveling abroad and asked to delay my Google second-round interviews by two weeks, and the team had no issue with that timeline.

Don't Give Them an Ultimatum

Although you need to fight your corner when it comes to salary, there's a point at which it can tip over into being aggressive. Nobody likes to be told "Do this or else," so try to avoid giving ultimatums even if you get frustrated. Ultimately, you want the company and employees to remain on good terms with you, as you could be working with them in this role or later on in your career.

Be Patient

Sometimes salary negotiations can take a while, and you may experience long delays in the process before you get confirmation of your formal offer. My salary negotiation process at Google actually took an entire month because the recruiter had to take my counteroffer numbers back to the compensation committee to get approval. You may think the employer is playing mind games or stringing you along, but if you're this far along in the process, these people like you and want to continue liking you. Stay in touch and be patient.

If you do chase them up, make sure to do it only once a week at the most, otherwise it'll seem desperate or pushy. If the recruiter gets back to you saying that they will reach back out to you, let them take the initiative to get in contact. Don't call up in frustration or anger. The best thing you can do is ask for clarification on timing, ask if there's anything you can do to help move things along, and then wait.

The only exception to this is if you have multiple offers and one is about to expire before the other. In this case, you should let the recruiter know about your situation and see if they can speed up the process for you. In parallel, you should talk to the hiring manager for the offer that is about to expire and try to extend the deadline. This way, you can buy yourself more time to make a decision.

Understanding Components of Salary

Compensation Outside of Your Base Salary

Your base salary is what you're paid every pay period. Usually, paydays are every other week. However, there are a lot of elements outside of your base salary that form your entire compensation package, or "total compensation" (TC). This could include the following:

Equity: This is your ownership stake in the company. Depending on the stage of the company and your role, this could easily be half of your total compensation (this is more likely at a small startup).

Benefits: This includes things like health insurance, vacation days, sick days, free food, and other perks. These are mostly untaxed.

Annual bonus: This is a percentage bonus on top of your salary, often based on performance, and is common only with public companies. Recruiters will usually quote a "target bonus" (e.g., 10 percent or 15 percent) which you'll get if you meet expectations. You may then receive a higher or lower percentage bonus based on appraisal of your work. This appraisal "rating" occurs every six months at Google.

Signing bonus: This is a one-time bonus that's paid out once you start the job. This may come with a clause that you must pay it back if you leave the company within a certain number of months (e.g., twelve months). This is very common in large tech companies, and signing bonuses can range between $10,000 and $50,000. In my experience, this component is highly negotiable. Even if the recruiter initially said there are no signing bonuses for the position, I've been able to secure one each time I've negotiated.

Relocation bonus: This is a one-time bonus that pays for moving costs. When you've been offered your dream job but it's in a different city, it's time to start thinking about relocation. Given that relocation costs can reach in the tens of thousands of dollars, you'll want to negotiate the best deal to make sure your move is as smooth and stress-free as possible.

Other perks: This could be any free or discounted benefits, such as a cell phone and plan, gym memberships, tuition reimbursement, commuter benefits, and more.

Understanding the Impact of Your "Level"

One of the biggest variables that controls your compensation is your internal "level" in the company, which is a number that expresses your seniority. For example, a level three at Meta (on the BizOps team) typically has three years of work experience, while a level four has four or five years of work experience. Make sure you check with your recruiter which level they've hired you for before you accept your offer! Do note that levels are not standard between companies, so make sure to do your research and ask current employees to see if you are leveled fairly.

In many tech companies, an employee's level is confidential, and other employees won't be able to tell which level you are once you've joined unless you tell them directly.

Understanding Equity as Compensation

Generally, all tech companies, small and large, offer equity but not always to all employees. It's often easier to negotiate for more equity than base salary.

Equity represents the value of the shares you own in the company. The company will never give you stock directly, because you'd have to pay taxes on it right away. Instead, companies have designed roundabout mechanisms to delay taxation. Restricted stock units (RSUs) are the most common way for larger companies to accomplish this.

RSUs are a form of equity compensation issued by an employer to an employee in the form of company shares. These are issued to an employee through a vesting plan and distribution schedule after the employee achieves required performance milestones or stays with the employer for a particular length of time.

RSUs don't have any tangible value until vesting is complete, and these units are assigned fair market value once they vest. Once vested, they are considered income, so you will pay income tax when the shares are delivered. Some company plans let you pay taxes by keeping a portion of the shares withheld to pay income taxes. As the employee, you receive the remaining shares and can sell them at your discretion. Therefore, the amount you're offered will not represent its actual value after taxes.

RSUs can also be subject to capital gains tax, but this would only apply to any gain in the stock price, after you sell the stock, that may have occurred after the stock was issued to you, creating a profit. For example, if you're issued $10,000's worth of RSUs as part of your compensation package, you will pay ordinary income tax on $10,000. If you choose to hold on to $5,000 worth of stock (not sell) and the stock increases to a value of $8,000, you will need to pay capital gains tax on the $3,000 value increase in addition to the ordinary income tax.

An employee stock purchase plan (ESPP) is a less common alternative that some tech companies use instead of RSUs. "An ESPP is a stock ownership plan that allows you to purchase shares of your company's stock, usually at a discount, with funds deducted from your paychecks," explains E-Trade.[29] "ESPP shares are yours as soon as the stock purchase is completed. You can hold on to

29 "Understanding Employee Stock Purchase Plans," E-Trade, February 28, 2019, https://us.etrade.com/knowledge/library/stock-plans/employee-stock-purchase-plan.

the shares as part of your portfolio or sell them at your discretion (subject to any employer-required holding period). Typically, only full-time, permanent employees are eligible to participate in an ESPP program."[30]

How to Do Salary Research and Benchmarking

It's worth doing research into average salaries for the roles you're applying for so that you can benchmark. You want to make sure that your offer is competitive internally and across the industry. Below are some key sources of information that I've found helpful. I recommend you use all of these or at least multiple sources to develop a comprehensive understanding of the industry and better prepare for salary negotiations.

Levels.fyi, Glassdoor, LinkedIn, and H1Bdata.info

Levels.fyi is a good place to start when doing salary research on tech companies. On levels.fyi, you can view salaries for different companies by position and level and filter them by skill, location, and years of experience.

I've found this more useful than Glassdoor since Glassdoor doesn't have granularity of data (meaning it's hard to distinguish between levels), and it's more difficult to benchmark your salary offer if you can't compare apples to apples. However, Glassdoor is broader, whereas levels.fyi is tech-industry specific.

LinkedIn is accurate for most common roles but not great for uncommon roles. On LinkedIn, you can also set up job alerts to stay updated with new job postings that match your preferences. You'll also have the flexibility to choose whether you want to re-

30 "Understanding Employee Stock Purchase Plans," E-Trade, February 28, 2019, https://us.etrade.com/knowledge/library/stock-plans/employee-stock-purchase-plan.

ceive these alerts on a daily or weekly basis through email, app notifications, or both.

Last, H1Bdata.info, also known as H1B Salary Database, is the best resource for international students. With Glassdoor and LinkedIn, you might be scrolling through jobs and not know which ones will sponsor you. With H1Bdata.info, you won't have that issue anymore. H1Bdata.info indexed more than four million H1-B salary records from the United States Department of Labor's disclosure data. You can sort by city, company, or job titles to see which ones have the highest number of H-1B visa filings and what the average salary is. Before you apply to a role, type in the company and job title to check if they've hired for your role.

Internal Company Forums

Internally at Google and Meta, there are anonymous forums where employees will share their salaries, level, and role. A good rule of thumb I heard from a coworker is that each promotion is generally around a 25 percent increase in total compensation. Thus, you should be able to calculate what your salary would be if you were to stay at Meta from a level three to a level six. Please note that this compensation percentage increase does drop as you keep climbing the corporate ladder. For years when you don't get promoted, you can expect a 3 to 10 percent increase in total compensation based on your ratings and time you've been at the company. For example, the percentage bump will be prorated if you've only been at the company for six months instead of the full year.

Professional Community Forums

Blind is another helpful resource when joining big tech companies. This app offers an anonymous forum and community for verified employees across all industries to discuss salaries and work issues. Do take it with a grain of salt, though, since those who are more willing to share are either doing really well or really poorly, and their experiences may not be representative of the average offer.

Current and Former Employees

Unfortunately, the best and most up-to-date information on salaries is a moving target, but it will be common knowledge among current employees. The best way for you to tap into that is by speaking with at least one person who is a current or former employee in a similar role you're interviewing for. This can take a little more research, time, and networking than the previous techniques, but it will probably give you a more accurate and useful answer.

Additional Benefits to Consider

Especially in Silicon Valley, many companies provide additional benefits or perks outside of your salary, 401(k), and health insurance. They are worth considering as important components of your compensation, as they can improve your quality of life day to day. The following are my favorite examples. Unless specified, these are offered by both Meta and Google:

- Free, healthy gourmet food for breakfast, lunch, and even dinner if you stay until 6:00 p.m. There are also coffee and juice bars scattered throughout the campuses. We're extremely well fed. Eating on campus saves time and money and also helps me build relationships with my coworkers.
- Free fitness classes and gyms on campus.
- Commuter subsidy. For example, Google pays $270 a month for mass transit and another $270 a month for parking.
- Game rooms with *Dance Dance Revolution*, *Street Fighter*, air

hockey, and more.

- On-site medical and dental staff, which means no more waiting for days or weeks to book time with your doctor.
- Shuttle buses to and from campus.
- A work cell phone and plan (which even includes reimbursement for international data for personal trips).
- The opportunity to beta test products that haven't been released yet.
- Exposure to amazing people and thinkers. I get to listen to and meet with people I grew up reading and being inspired by. For example, we invited speakers such as Michelle Obama and Jonny Kim to speak at Google.
- Tuition reimbursement. At Google there's two-thirds reimbursement for job-related tuition expenses, and one-third reimbursement for personal expenses. I've been able to get partially reimbursed for cooking and dance classes!
- Off-site events for team bonding! For example, wine tasting, curling, go-kart racing, aquarium visits, white-water rafting, and so on.
- Death benefit. This one is a bit morbid, but if a Googler passes away while working there, all their stock vests immediately, and, on top of the life insurance payout, their surviving spouse continues to get half of the Googler's salary for the next ten years. There's also an additional $1,000 per month benefit for any of the Googler's children.
- Baby cash. At Meta, reimbursement of $4,000 for every new parent and up to $3,000 in babysitting funds each year are available.

- On-site laundry.

- Maternity and paternity leave. At Meta, there are sixteen weeks of paid maternity and paternity leave. At Google, parental leave is eighteen weeks for all parents and at least twenty-four weeks for all parents who give birth. In addition, there's a two-week "ramp-up" period at Google, when parents can work part-time at full pay after returning from parental leave.

- Paid time off (PTO). At Meta, I started with twenty-one PTO days, and at Google it's twenty PTO days (which builds up over time). In light of COVID-19, Google also gave additional mental health days off in order to support Googlers' well-being.

- Volunteering time. You are given twenty hours a year of paid leave to dedicate to volunteering, and Google also matches your donations to any eligible organizations up to $10,000.

15

How to Succeed Once You Land the Role

Congratulations! You've landed your dream job as a strategist working with a team you love on a product you're passionate about. But now what? This probably felt like the final step, but it's only the beginning. Now the real work starts. This is your opportunity to nurture a healthy and long-lasting career in the industry, and it's worth having a strategy that will help you to make the most of it while navigating the inevitable pressures and obstacles.

No one sets out to fail at a job, but it can happen if you don't take the time to establish good habits from your first day in the new position. The good news is that succeeding in your role is largely under your control!

In this chapter, I'll cover tips for career ramp-up and advancement, finding a mentor, creating work-life balance, and how to give and receive feedback. These factors can all influence your professional growth and contribute to your future impact and success.

Ramping Up Quickly as a "Noogler" or "N00b"

New hires at Google and Meta are called "Nooglers" or "n00bs" respectively. This title indicates that you're still onboarding and learning the ropes. Enjoy the beginning. It's a wonderful honeymoon period! During this phase, you get to meet lots of new people and earn new processes, and the workload is typically low. Here are just a few tips I'd recommend during this six-month period to ramp up quickly and gain traction.

Learn the Lingo

Tech companies such as Google and Meta have their own language, and you can feel like an outsider until you get to grips with it. It will take time, but it helps if, during meetings, you keep a sheet of acronyms and technologies that you don't know, creating your own dictionary of terms. Then when you get back to your desk, find out what they are and keep a note for next time. At Meta, there is an internal dictionary called "Wut" to look up these acronyms. At Google, the internal dictionary is called "WTF."

General lore is that those lists tend to grow for the first six months. Learning about one acronym will generally have a domino effect and add another five to six more items to the list. Don't worry—the list will start shrinking after a couple of months of ramping up.

You will find that most of your colleagues in strategy-type roles will come from consulting backgrounds. This has its own lingo that you'll need to get to grips with too. Here is a helpful reference to understand the most commonly used terms:

10,000-ft view: This means to zoom out from the details of the problem and think more like a high-level executive.

Adding value: This is simply the value that is being added to an effort or project.

Bird's-eye view: A higher-level perspective, similar to how birds see things from above.

Boil the ocean: This indicates that you're taking on too much at once. You will hear "Let's not boil the ocean" if someone is suggesting a lot of analyses that will make a job or project unnecessarily difficult.

Double click: Conduct a deeper investigation of a certain area.

Deliverable: The final product you deliver at the end of a project.

Low-hanging fruit: The easiest-to-implement opportunities.

MECE: Mutually exclusive, collectively exhaustive (see my definition in chapter 12).

Buy-in: Support or agreement from stakeholders.

EOD: End of day. However, this could mean 5:00 p.m. local time, midnight, or before I get into work tomorrow, depending on the person.

Takeaway: Important point or action item from a meeting.

80/20: Eighty percent of a business problem can be solved by focusing on 20 percent of the causal factors, so finish 80 percent of an assignment in 20 percent of the time instead of completing 100 percent (I go into more detail on this later in the chapter).

Let me play this back: Let me repeat what was said to see if we're aligned.[31]

Don't Be Afraid to Speak Up

As a new employee, you have a fresh perspective as you haven't drunk the Kool-Aid (yet). Use it to your advantage! Don't shy away just because you're new: speak up and present your perspective. If you're not sure how your team would respond to feedback, frame your observations as questions instead. For example, instead of

31 "The Management Consulting Lingo Dictionary," Management Consulted, accessed October 25, 2020, https://managementconsulted.com/about/dictionary/.

suggesting that constant forecasting might be getting in the way of creative work, you might instead ask: "This might be a n0Ob question, but I was wondering why we have four forecasting cycles each year?"

Be Smart about When to Ask for Help

Google and Meta can be intimidating places for newcomers since you'll be surrounded by a lot of smart people. A common pitfall for n0Obs and Nooglers is to not ask questions early on since they are too concerned about being perceived as "not smart enough." They try to figure out too many things by themselves. As a result, they cannot move fast enough. At the same time, if you do not spend time researching and always go directly to people to find out the answer, you will miss great learning opportunities and will probably fail to gain respect from your coworkers. I've heard that the "thirty minutes" rule is great for new members. When you run into a problem, spend thirty minutes trying to figure it out by yourself. If, after thirty minutes, you have no clue, you should go and ask for help.

Tips and Tricks for Career Advancement

In college, working hard equated to getting good grades and succeeding. However, it's not necessarily the same in the real world. Working hard will help you be successful in your career, but it's not enough. What's equally important is how you work, whom you work with, and what projects you work on. While you're building your career, keep these tips in mind.

Become an Expert in One Area

When you first join a team, it can be tempting to pass all the questions to other people since they know so much more and have been at the company longer than you. However, when you do that, you're not adding a lot of value.

Instead, try to quickly find one area where you can become the expert and really take the time to understand that space and the customers. Think about what research you need to do to get to grips with it. For example, my area of expertise is third-party advertiser acquisitions at Google. We either acquire new advertisers to Google directly through Google's sales teams or through third-party agencies, and I specialize in the agency side. I made it my goal in the first few months of ramping up to become the "go-to" expert on agency questions. During this time, I shadowed agency development managers (salespeople) to understand what advertisers are looking for. I looked through the data and metrics and talked to as many stakeholders as I could. I also chatted with the previous analyst in this role to learn the background from my team.

When you do your homework, you can make decisions more confidently and become a valuable asset to the team!

Look for a Team Where You Can Pick up New Skills

If you've mostly worked on mature products, consider joining a team where you can work on a new, unlaunched product. While I was working at Facebook, I was focused on the most mature product (Facebook Newsfeed), but I made an effort to expand into areas like Instant Articles and Facebook Stories since those were newer products with different challenges. If you've always worked on consumer products, you could consider working on business-facing products instead. Examine your skillset to pinpoint the gaps, and then find a place to learn those skills on the job.

Choose the Company Where You'll Learn the Most

At different stages of your career, you'll want to learn different things. To optimize your learning, you'll need to choose a company that will support you in that stage of your growth. If you're brand new to BizOps or the tech industry, you'll want to learn the basics, and it would benefit you to pick a company with several strong BizOps leaders to learn from or a larger company that leads in the industry where you can learn the gold standard.

On the other hand, once you've been a BizOps analyst or associate for some time, you might want to consider increasing your responsibilities, scope, and independence, and it could be helpful to pick a smaller company to do that. Working in a startup means that you're an important member of a small team. This leads to more responsibility and authority to make decisions and will give you a new type of challenge and more opportunities to branch out into other fields.

Most startups have blurred boundaries between different roles and functions, which allows employees to perform multiple jobs at the same time. You might have to wear different hats—you could be a BizOps analyst, a marketer, and a product manager all at the same time. Switching between different roles and juggling responsibilities not only makes you more aware of your capabilities but also allows you to explore different functions of your industry early in your career.

Find a Manager Who Believes in You

When choosing a team, don't just look at the product; make sure you also consider who your manager will be. Your manager can really make or break your experience, and many great BizOps leaders credit their success to managers who gave them opportunities to prove themselves.

By talking to current employees at the company, you can start to learn who the best managers are and who are the ones to avoid. Once you have a good manager, show them that you're reliable and can do good work. Then, have a conversation about how you want your career to grow, and be brave enough to take on the challenges they give to you.

I've listed some good signs and red flags below that should help you to assess a manager's behavior. If you notice any of these red flags, it might be time to start thinking about switching teams or managers or even bringing up these issues with your skip level (your manager's manager).

Good Signs

- Follows up and checks in after you've shared a personal problem.
- Remembers a personal event, name, or detail.
- Says hello and checks in (even if just over online chat) multiple times a week.
- Proactively mentions an opportunity you should explore.
- Gives you their whole attention during one-on-one meetings (1:1s).
- Gives you credit when your work is highlighted.
- Shows real understanding of your unique needs.
- Admits and proactively shares their mistakes.
- Encourages you to speak up and raise challenges.
- Plans for the future and helps create a career roadmap with milestones.
- Ensures that their employees are happy or at least satisfied with their work.
- Keeps in touch when you leave their team.

Red Flags

- Cancels 1:1s regularly or last minute.
- Doesn't immediately have your back when a colleague makes a complaint about you.
- Ignores your emails or pings.
- Doesn't say hello regularly or make eye contact.
- Always brings the conversation back to themselves (especially in career and performance discussions).
- Uses phones and laptops during 1:1s (for unrelated tasks).
- Talks about their own chances of promotion.
- Makes you feel uncomfortable speaking up or challenging decisions.
- Presents your work as theirs.
- Stays in their office most of the time with the door closed.
- Gossips about peers to you.
- Has "favorites" on the team.

In many internal consulting roles, you'll work with a manager and a lead. For example, I report directly to my strategy and operations manager at Google, but I work more closely with a team of program managers and their lead. Both your manager and your lead will influence your time significantly at the company, so you should look for similar good qualities in your lead.

Focus on Your Own Efficiency

Prepare to be bombarded with tasks or requests as an analyst. You'll need to know what you can drop if needed. You'll want to be responsive to your team and not be the one who creates a bottleneck, so it's important to prioritize how you spend your time to make the most impact.

One agile way to prioritize tasks is to (1) identify the time, duration, and complexity it will take to do the work, and (2) identify the business value of that work. Then, categorize (1) and (2) into T-shirt sizes: XS, S, M, L, XL. As you might expect, when you're categorizing (1), XS relates to a very quick and simple task, and XL relates to a long, complex, and intensive task. When you're categorizing (2), XS means that it doesn't have much value for the business, while XL means significant value. The sizes can, if needed, be given numerical values after the estimation is done. This is a very informal technique, but it can be used quickly with a large number of items in order to help you prioritize work that requires little time but is high impact.

When I first joined Google, my biggest mistake was saying yes to every request, even when it was just a data point that someone was curious about and wasn't going to take any action upon. Make sure you understand the hypothesis before digging into data. This will make you more efficient and effective. Now, my first instinct is to ask questions before saying yes or no to a request. I assess the priority of the task by asking what the context is and understanding how the data will be used to influence a decision or action. If I think the potential impact is limited and I have other tasks on my plate that are high priority, I might reply and explain that it's not in my best interests to take this on. If they insist, we can set up time with my manager to determine if reprioritization is needed.

Some people have found "inbox zero" to be an effective technique to increase efficiency. This is a philosophy developed by the productivity expert Merlin Mann that encourages you to manage your inbox so that it doesn't overwhelm and use up all of your creative energy. You aim to keep your inbox closed for most of the day, and when you do open it, you respond to all emails that will only take two minutes to deal with and process the rest with either *delete, delegate, respond, defer,* or *do.* Even making small changes to your routine can make a big difference in how organized you are. I've made sure to block out "focus times" on my calendar when I can get work done without distraction. Many of us spend time switching between tasks, like between an analysis and a meeting, but you can't do your best work when your attention is scattered in this way. Psychologist Dr. David Meyer "has said that even brief mental blocks created by shifting between tasks can cost as much as 40 percent of someone's productive time."[32] Thus, in focusing on one task for a sustained period of time, I've reduced the need for constant context switching.

Help Your Team with Something Tangible Early On

As a new analyst at a company, you need to prove yourself, and it's best to do that early on. This is made more difficult by the fact that most of the tasks you'll undertake will be behind the scenes, so your coworkers might not actually see how hard you work. Look around your team and find some grunt work you can take off someone's plate. For example, at Facebook we had a daily email on Facebook App revenue trends to keep leadership up to date on our performance and our financial outlook. I offered to take this off my manager's plate since it was a manual and repetitive task. This not only got me more familiar with the datasets, but it also gave me a lot of visibility in the company. I was sending emails to leaders such as Fidji Simo (then head of Facebook App), and others complimented me on how quickly I ramped up and started to make an

32 "Multitasking: Switching Costs," American Psychological Association, March 20, 2006, https://www.apa.org/research/action/multitask.

impact. Doing this type of work will get you off to a good start with your team and earn you goodwill that'll help you in the future!

Demonstrate That You Consistently Deliver Work at the Next Level

Most established, larger companies will have a documented career ladder and skills needed at each level. These ladders can be frustrating because they seem concrete and explicit, and yet you can meet all of the requirements for your current level without being promoted.

Here's the thing. You need to meet not only all the requirements for your current level but also all the requirements for the next level before being promoted to it. Not only that, you need to earn a reputation for consistently delivering work at that next level. One tip I suggest is to pull out the company rubric to see how you measure up against the requirements for the next level. Check in with your manager to see if you're accurately identifying any weaker areas that you need to work on in order to get there. Then focus on those areas and regularly get feedback to make sure you're making progress. Last, volunteer to share and present your work at team meetings so that other peers and leaders can vouch for your great work.

Define and Measure Your Own Success

One way you can stand out is to be more concrete about what your success means and how you'll measure it. On certain projects, success will mean increasing incremental revenue, user growth, or increased engagement. For others, success might mean having better customer satisfaction survey results.

Once you've decided on these metrics for success, communicate them to your manager and team and keep track of their status so that they can easily see when you're hitting your targets. I typically have a green, yellow, or red symbol next to each KPI in order to hold myself accountable and understand if I'm on track or not.

Build Your Personal Brand

Personal branding is the process by which we market ourselves to others. Your personal brand comprises (1) internal attributes, (2) self-perception, and (3) external perception. Even if you have great internal attributes, such as relationship building or strategy planning, you won't get credit for these at work if people do not perceive you the same way you perceive yourself.

One helpful method for thinking about your brand is through the Johari window. The Johari window is one framework to identify where there may be any gaps in the perception of yourself. This framework was created by psychologists Joseph Luft and Harrington Ingham in 1955, and it is now a very popular team-building exercise at Google.

Below you'll see the Johari window.[33] As you can see, there are four quadrants, and each one represents information about you. Two of these panes represent self, and the other two represent the parts unknown to the self but known to others.

	Known to self	Not known to self
Known to others	**Open self** Conscious actions and statements known to you and others.	**Unaware self** Things others know about you of which you may not be aware.
Not known to others	**Hidden self** Things you know about yourself and choose to keep to yourself.	**Unknown self** Things about you that are not known to you or others (yet!).

33 Joseph Luft and Harrington Ingham, "The Johari Window: A Graphic Model of Interpersonal Awareness," *Proceedings of the Western Training Laboratory in Group Development* (Los Angeles: UCLA, 1955).

When you build trust with your coworkers, you'll be able to gather feedback and feel more comfortable sharing about yourself. Thus, as time goes on, there will be more information transfer within these panes. For example, when I first started working in a corporate environment, I was shy, kept my head down, and did good work. However, because I didn't share my learnings more broadly in group settings, people didn't know that I was a great analyst. I had a huge "hidden self" pane. I was also too afraid to ask for feedback and didn't want to hear anything negative, so I had a large "unaware self" pane as well.

Recently, I've gotten better at sharing my work more broadly, and I thus get better acknowledgment for the work I do. My "hidden self" pane has shrunk. I'm also more comfortable asking for feedback, so I'm able to improve and shrink the "unknown self" pane. My "open self" pane has continued to grow and overshadow the other panes, and that's ideally what should happen when you're building your personal brand.

Now, let's do a quick exercise. Try writing a personal brand statement to identify your strengths and values. You can do this by asking close friends and family to describe you using adjectives.

[Name] is [adjective, adjective, and adjective]. She's known for [. . .] and is the go-to person for [. . .].

My example: *Mari is driven, scrappy, and data-oriented. She's known for being eager to learn new things and is the go-to person for SQL-related questions.*

Now that you have your brand statement, how do you *manage* your brand? Work your way through the five components below that tackle defining, shaping, and promoting your brand.

Perception

- What is one strength that people say you have?

- What is one strength you would want people to say you had?
- What can you start or stop doing to manage people's perceptions?

Visibility

- How can you increase your visibility?
- What can you do to promote your work? One way I do this is by volunteering to present my work regularly at staff meetings.

Uniqueness

- How are you different from the person sitting next to you?
- What is it about you that few people can duplicate?
- How is this relevant to your audience? It's no secret that different people want different things. What can you bring to the table that will resonate the most with your audience?

Packaging

- Are you dressing for who you want to be?
- What does your workspace say about you? Although it's wise to avoid judging someone's workspace, people often do so when it's on display in an open plan office. Colleagues may perceive that you are less conscientious and productive with a cluttered workspace.

- How well do you communicate and present your ideas?
- In what other ways can your appearance help or hinder you?
- What is your body language (e.g., hand gestures, eye movements, posture, facial expressions) saying about you? For example, when in meetings, think about how your body language can influence not only the external but also the internal aspects of your personal brand, like your own confidence. How we hold our bodies can have an impact on our minds. In other words, by having a powerful stance, we can actually make ourselves feel more powerful and confident.

Relationships

- Who are your main stakeholders? For example, are you mostly working with technical or non-technical folks? If you're trying to talk to a data engineer, you can probably share your SQL script and go into more technical details. If you're sharing your work with a senior executive, you'll want to present how your analysis will impact business growth or prioritization. You can demonstrate your data savviness in different ways to different audiences.
- What is their preferred working style? For example, some prefer email to meetings in terms of communication style. If you can adapt to the communication style of your audience, your message will likely be received better.
- How can you expand your network?

Hopefully these questions will help you brainstorm how to manage your brand more intentionally going forward!

Communicate Frequently

In order to be on the same page as your team lead and manager, you need to spend time with them. There is no shortcut. Getting more time on their calendars gives you the opportunity to get into the details and stay on the same page.

If you don't already have weekly 1:1s with your team lead and manager, I would recommend asking if you can schedule them to get more face time. In addition to these weekly 1:1s, I also set up monthly career chats with my manager to make sure I'm tracking toward my longer-term career goals. Finally, I set up a sync between the three of us (me, the team lead, and my manager) at the beginning of each quarter to align on my objectives and key results (OKR). Frequent communication can help make sure that both your team lead and manager have a good understanding of what you are spending your time on and agree that it is valuable.

Find a Mentor

People in BizOps have all different skills. Some people are better at broader strategic thinking, while others are good at structured communication or data analysis. Identify people who you think are very strong in an area you want to improve in, and reach out to them.

Be specific when you reach out to a mentor about what you need. Maybe you want to run a deck skeleton by them to make sure it's structured, or maybe you want to show them your opportunity sizing formula and get their feedback. Being purposeful makes the relationship work well for both of you.

In the next section, we'll go over more details on how to find a mentor.

How to Find a Mentor

Imagine this scenario: A person you admire sets time aside for the two of you to meet, shares how she accomplished her goals, cheers you on, and gives you feedback and advice. We'd all want this in our lives, wouldn't we? This is what we call a mentor!

A mentor can be your manager or someone completely outside of your team and company. Mentorship is sharing knowledge, skills, and life experience to guide another toward reaching their full potential. Mentoring can be powerful—"it can lead to a new job, a promotion, or even a better work-life balance."[34] The toughest part is finding and asking for mentorship. I get it; it's difficult to ask for advice and seek out assistance from others. But the truth is asking for help from others can be very beneficial to your performance, development, and career progression, so it's worth making the uncomfortable request.

Here are some tips for finding the right mentor, asking for what you want, and making the relationship work!

Finding the Right Mentor

Think about what your professional career goals look like. Do you want a promotion? Do you wish to become a people manager? Do you want to be CEO?

Where do you want to be in five years? Ten years? What about when you retire? When you've mapped out those milestones, the next step is to look for people who have achieved these goals in their own careers.

The best place to start is your own network. Write down a list of previous managers, coworkers, friends, or family members who are in your target industry or dream role. It can help to scroll through

34 Anjuli Sastry Krbechek and Andee Tagle, "The Right Mentor Can Change Your Career. Here's How to Find One," NPR, September 3, 2020, https://www.npr.org/2019/10/25/773158390/how-to-find-a-mentor-and-make-it-work.

your Facebook and LinkedIn contacts. Is there someone you admire or want to emulate? Usually, the people you've worked with will know your strengths and weaknesses, and they'll be able to help in areas you may be lacking knowledge or skills in. These seasoned professionals will be able to look at your career from a different perspective and give you tactical advice on how to navigate your own path. If the person you want as a mentor wouldn't ordinarily cross paths with you, take action to purposely find a way to connect. For example, I decided to take on planning social events at work because the lead for that initiative was someone I wanted as a mentor. You may find that your future mentor is not in your immediate circle of friends, but that's okay too. Utilize your first-degree connections to provide warm introductions to your prospective mentors.

Asking for What You Want

First, organize your thoughts and figure out what you want from the mentor-mentee relationship. Next, do your research. If you haven't met, mention what you like about the person's background or work. Doing your research will show that you're thoughtful about your approach to finding a mentor.

Prep what you're going to say ahead of time, and make sure to practice in front of a mirror or record yourself. You want to make a good impression, especially if it's your first time meeting this person. You may want to start out with a casual coffee chat before you pop the question to your prospective mentor.[35]

Last and most important, try making this ask in person. While it's not always possible, it's best to meet in person to ask for formal mentorship.

---

35 Krbechek and Tagle, "The Right Mentor Can Change Your Career. Here's How to Find One."

Making the Relationship Work

Send an agenda before the meeting. It's always a good idea to set an agenda, as this can help prevent meetings from veering off track. An effective agenda will set clear expectations for what needs to occur before and during a meeting. That way, your mentor will have adequate time to prepare and allocate time for the topics you want to cover during the meeting.

Set up recurring meetings, and check to see what cadence works well for the two of you. Most of my mentors and I meet monthly for half an hour each session, but everyone has a different preference. For the initial meet-and-greet, I prefer meeting in person, but then I've gradually transitioned to video conferencing or phone calls from there.[36]

Take notes. Your mentor is likely a busy person, and documenting your meetings with dated notes will help to remind both of you of what you discussed and make sure you're on track for future discussions.[37]

Ask for feedback. Feedback can be positive or constructive! It's good to get a healthy serving of tough feedback among the compliments because it will help you grow and evolve and, ultimately, achieve your goals.[38] I'll go into more detail on how to ask for feedback later in this chapter.

Give back. Instead of just asking for mentorship, I've learned to give back too: "How can I help you?" or "Hey, I have someone I want to introduce you to." When you offer something genuinely interesting, you're proving your value. In return, you'll get the

36 Krbechek and Tagle, "The Right Mentor Can Change Your Career. Here's How to Find One."

37 Krbechek and Tagle, "The Right Mentor Can Change Your Career. Here's How to Find One."

38 Krbechek and Tagle, "The Right Mentor Can Change Your Career. Here's How to Find One."

mentorship, the recommendation letter, or the speaking opportunity that you've always wanted.

How can you apply this if you're a student? Let's say your mentor mentioned that they want to get more speaking opportunities. You could say, "I'm a part of the business club on campus and would be delighted to welcome you as a virtual speaker this semester." This way it can be a mutually beneficial relationship.

As a student, you're valuable to employers and mentors, but I hope you realize that you're also valuable, period. Don't let anyone treat you "less than" just because they have a fat paycheck or forty years of experience. You have every right to offer your value to people you like and to say no to whomever you want.

Tips for Presenting to Senior Leaders

Senior leaders are one of the toughest crowds you'll face as a presenter. They are demanding, they are time poor, and they don't want to sit still for a long presentation with a big reveal at the end. If your presentation is short and insightful, it will land well and they will be willing to listen to you next time. More importantly, giving impressive presentations to senior leaders is a great way to improve your visibility in the company and your chances of promotion.

The advice on creating impactful slides in chapter 12 will help you a great deal, but here are some specific tips that will help you make the right impression with leadership.

Focused and Minimal Slides

Send slides and materials in advance—preferably two days ahead—and ask senior leaders to read them before the meeting. At the start of the meeting, verify if they have read the materials and check how they want to proceed.

Where appropriate, include a set of discussion questions and begin the discussion there rather than taking a tour of the deck. This can be helpful if the audience has already read the deck in advance and wants to jump directly into questions.

Know your key takeaways by heart. What is the story? Do your slides support the story?

Limit the number of slides and use your appendix wisely. Don't include slides in the main deck if you will skip through them, as you'll lose the audience's attention.

Clear and Defined Goals and Purpose

Identify what problem you are solving and state it up front.

Be clear and specific about what you want out of the meeting—"We need two engineers who can do X" or "We need more resources"—then frame the discussion to get that to happen. If useful, specify topics that are in scope versus out of scope for the purposes of the meeting and your needs.

Think about your audience. What is their POV? What is most important to them? What is likely to be on their mind today? How can you ensure the presentation speaks to that?

If a leader has invited you to present, make sure you understand in advance exactly what they and their team are hoping to get from you.

Thorough Preparation and Practice

If possible, have someone prepare the leader in advance for the presentation. For example, ask your manager to check with the leader: "This meeting is coming up on topic X, and we'd like your input on Y. Any thoughts as we prepare those materials?"

If you will be one of multiple presenters, choreograph what each presenter will cover and how you will manage handoffs. If a co-presenter fails to show up, are you prepared to step in? Be prepared to run the whole meeting yourself. Do you know the numbers so you can cite them instead of flipping through to find the right slide? If time runs short, can you quickly summarize? If and when the group goes off on tangents, can you bring them back to the key theme?

Do a mock presentation with your team as well as a practice Q and A session, and anticipate what you will do if there are surprises or problems.

Don't bring people to the presentation who won't actually be presenting or who are not essential to the discussion. This could waste their time and potentially derail your conversation.

Be prepared for surprises. Show that you can adapt and that you know your stuff. Think through different scenarios and how you will react creatively and professionally. For example, what if they say, "Just show us one slide"? What if they engage in small talk? Be prepared to follow their lead briefly to build rapport, and then determine the best way to bring focus back to the topic at hand. What if their agenda has changed and you only have five minutes instead of the thirty minutes you planned on? Consider creating backup slides for potential challenges, difficult questions, trade-offs, or alternative solutions.

Automate the Boring Tasks

As an analyst, you will inevitably have some operational work, and this will usually be repetitive. If you've ever spent hours renaming files or updating hundreds of spreadsheet cells, you know how tedious tasks like these can be. But what if you could have your computer do them for you? Automating can free up your time for more creative and big picture tasks, which will help you shine. You will also be bringing more efficiency to the company's work, and it'll demonstrate that you can take initiative and problem-solve independently. These will all help you succeed in your role.

For example, at Google we have weekly revenue calls set up with sales leadership. While this work is necessary to keep leaders up to date on how the business is trending, it can also be repetitive and boring to update the slides each week. Therefore, our team has automated as much of it as possible.

We connected our SQL script directly to Google Sheets so that when the SQL table updates each week with the latest revenue figures, we just need to click "refresh" on Google Sheets.[39] Then, we pasted the tables directly into Google Slides and selected the option to "link to spreadsheet." Therefore, every week, the only thing I need to do is press refresh on the spreadsheet, and Google Slides and all the latest numbers will populate. From there, I just add in commentary. You'll make your own life a lot easier if you automate the tasks that you do over and over!

If you want to get even more technically savvy and automate things like sending reminder emails, check out automatetheboringstuff.com or the book *Automate the Boring Stuff with Python* by Al Sweigart. "Even if you've never written a line of code, you can make your computer do the grunt work," writes Sweigart. His book teaches "how to use Python to write programs that do in minutes what would take you hours to do by hand—no prior programming experience required. Once you've mastered the basics of programming, you'll create Python programs that effortlessly perform useful and impressive feats of automation."[40] I highly recommend checking this out and trying it for yourself.

Create Work-Life Balance

Work-life balance is critical for maintaining good mental health and productivity. When the balance is off and you're spending too much time worrying about work, you will likely feel stressed

39 Learn how to use Connected Sheets here: https://cloud.google.com/bigquery/docs/connected-sheets.

40 Al Sweigart, "Automate the Boring Stuff with Python," accessed December 12, 2021, https://automatetheboringstuff.com/.

and burnt out. However, you can't just focus on improving your work life since that is only one side of the equation. What you do outside work matters as well. Finding that personal fulfillment through hobbies or volunteering is also crucial for striking that balance. You have a finite amount of time, energy, and resources, so be intentional about what you focus your time on, and do something that energizes you.

I'd also like to note that this balance is ever-changing and evolving, so be aware how your priorities shift, and make changes accordingly. For example, when you have your first child, you'll likely want to allocate more time to family so you can be there to witness your baby's first claps, steps, and other milestones.

I've listed some tips below that have helped me create work-life balance. I've also included guidance for finding balance when working remotely; this can throw different challenges into the mix, as there's little demarcation between home and work life.

Tips for Finding Balance

Follow the 80/20 rule.

The 80/20 rule, also known as the Pareto principle, will help you get the most out of the least amount of effort. It suggests that, typically, only 20 percent of your activities will account for 80 percent of the outcome. A small number of actions drive the vast majority of the results. Pareto originally thought about this concept in terms of land. He noticed 20 percent of Italy's population owned 80 percent of the land. In business, this principle can be applied to time management as well.

This rule will force you to invest your time more wisely and know when to stop. If you've already solved 20 percent of the issue to deliver 80 percent of the impact, you will begin realizing diminishing returns from any further effort. If 80 percent of the answer is enough, you can move on to something else, or you can focus on pushing the answer further at some other time.

Only attend meetings that are helpful.

Draw boundaries. Politely excuse yourself from meetings that you don't need to be part of (and check with your manager if that's okay). It's completely acceptable to devote your attention to activities that are the best use of your time. Create a rhythm that supports and sustains you.

Make time for one thing you love to do every day.

It's easy to get sucked into the whirlwind and let every day go by. One way to bring balance back into your life is to recommit to doing things that provide you with the most happiness. This could include walking, meditating, learning an instrument or language, reading, cooking, baking, and so on. It doesn't matter what it is as long as you get pleasure from the experience! In Marie Kondo's words, does it "spark joy"? If so, carve out time every day to do this one thing and do it consistently for thirty or more days to make it a habit.

Make time for family.

Create space to spend more time with the people that matter. This is different for every person but could include making sure you're home for family dinner or attending your daughter's soccer game.

Learn how to say no.

It is important that you actively plan what you want to spend your time doing or who you spend it with. On a day-to-day basis, you'll get many more requests and opportunities to do different things than are possible to complete. If you're passively agreeing to all the requests that come your way, you'll end up not having time for the important things that actually matter.

For example, I often get requests to look into a metric or do a deep dive just because someone is "curious." If a leader is curious but there's no clear action that will result from this knowledge, you can either (1) point them to a dashboard and teach them to self-pull the data, (2) point them to a different person who can do this, or (3) tell them to speak with your manager if they need to prioritize this. Your manager should be helping you push back on requests that don't have any actionable results, and you may have to ask for their backup at times.

Take time off to recharge.

Make sure to take time off to rest and recharge.[41] This is one of the best ways to create an environment for future high productivity and creativity. I used to save unused vacation days, let them accumulate, and roll them over to the next year. However, I found that this method quickly led to burnout. Now, I make it a point to use my paid time off and get some healthy space away from the office to relax. Take the time to prioritize your well-being and invest in yourself, and you'll feel so much happier and healthier. Now get out your calendar and mark down those rest days!

Tips for Working Remotely

Following the coronavirus pandemic, many companies are allowing flexible working weeks (e.g., Google allows three days in the office and two days at home) or even moving to a 100 percent remote model. Work-life balance is especially tough to achieve while working from home. The first thing to realize is that work-life balance varies from person to person and can change on a daily basis, so there are no right or wrong answers to how to achieve this. It can also vary drastically depending on whether you're single or

41 Mark Pettit, "13 Work Life Balance Tips for a Happy and Productive Life," Lifehack, accessed November 15, 2020, https://www.lifehack.org/734028/work-life-balance-tips.

married or have kids at home all day. Here are some tips I've found helpful.

Take a proper lunch break.

With easy access to the kitchen and no team to meet up with, you might be compelled to snack all day rather than take time out for lunch, but that won't help your productivity or sense of work-life balance. Make sure to set aside time to take a proper lunch break. You can do this by setting a calendar block or phone reminder for half an hour each day. Alternatively, you could schedule a virtual lunch break with the team so you can connect with each other while enjoying lunch!

"Go home" on time.

As much as I hate commuting, at least it signals the beginning and end of the work day. It can be tough to determine when to get up and walk away from your desk when you no longer have to worry about traffic or picking up children on time. However, it shouldn't change your schedule. Decide what time you finish up for the day and stick to it! Judge your productivity by your results rather than the hours you put in.

Sometimes I get emails after hours because my coworkers live in different time zones. In the past, I would respond right away, but now I make it a point to set my boundaries by waiting to respond until the next morning.

Exercise.

Exercise has many proven benefits, and it's an excellent way to achieve work-life balance while working from home. It reduces stress, pumps up your endorphins, and lifts your mood. If you don't have an hour in your schedule, just start with a fifteen-minute yoga stretch. If you can, find a type of exercise that seems fun rather than a chore. This can give you an added sense of accomplishment and self-care.

There are lots of free resources available online: CorePower Yoga, Barry's Bootcamp on Instagram Live, Planet Fitness's Facebook page, and YouTube channels (my personal favorites are Pamela Reif, Caroline Girvan, and Chloe Ting).

It also helps me when I make plans during weekday evenings. I register and pre-pay for my dance classes Tuesday and Thursday evenings, and they serve as a forcing function for me to get up from my desk and physically disengage from work.

Socialize.

It can be lonely to work from home. Random social interactions in the office help break up the day and make it unique; otherwise it feels like all the days are blending together.

You can combat this feeling by talking to your colleagues a couple times throughout the day. Schedule video coffee breaks, ask your colleagues what they did on the weekend, catch up on their family life, discuss what you're watching on Netflix, or play games together (my favorites are Skribbl and Codenames). It might feel strange to be taking time out from work like this, but you'd be enjoying these small breaks if you were in the office. These small interactions will go a long way to maintaining your work-life balance while working remotely.

Goal Setting

At Facebook, I set my individual goals every six months with my manager. I've included the template I used below. For goals that I was on track to hit, I marked them with a check symbol. For those that had roadblocks, I marked them as a flat line. For those that we decided to scrap or reprioritize for later, I marked them with a thick X. This allowed me to easily see what progress I was making and what I needed to focus on next. Feel free to use this to structure your own personal goals at work.

Objective Type	Work Team Objectives	Amy's Goals
Team/ Talent	Target, attract, and develop the best talent and create a positive culture for all team members.	• Help organize and attend team-related events (e.g., team lunches, ice cream, Q4 off-site planning). ✔ • Take time to invest in learning (e.g., BizCamp, Delivery Camp, Mark Q and As, Women's Leadership Summit). ✔ • Help ramp Mike to the team by hosting teach-ins for Newsfeed and IA. ✔

Objective Type	Work Team Objectives	Amy's Goals
Work	• Continuously improve our processes and practices to deliver higher quality and greater efficiency. • Develop robust product goals and help the business achieve them through accurate forecasting and tracking/management. • Make the business run better by delivering strategic projects that inform high-impact business decisions.	Achieve "exceeds expectations" rating by doing the following: • **Build variance reporting/tracking processes (mobile feed) and create a playbook to capture the process**—Take action independently in (1) following key product developments on Workplace; (2) getting experiment results from Deltoid; (3) reporting variances in a systematic and rigorous way in the ongoing weekly variance quips, the monthly revenue docs, and the earnings docs; and (4) outlining the process in a playbook and getting input from other people. ✔ • **Improve communication skills**—Communicate in a clear and concise way in presentations without reading off a script in the monthly revenue reviews, and make it clear when there are knowledge gaps. ✔ • **Build strong relationships with Data Science leads**—Build relationships that allow me and the team to be more successful. ✗ • **Project-based "state of market" work**—Publish a "state of the market" note so our team can showcase our work and broaden our impact. ✔

Work	• Continuously improve our processes and practices to deliver higher quality and greater efficiency. • Develop robust product goals and help the business achieve them through accurate forecasting and tracking/management. • Make the business run better by delivering strategic projects that inform high-impact business decisions.	• **Data tools**—Take Udemy's "Beginner to Pro in Excel: Financial Modeling and Valuation" course in order to be more efficient in Excel. Work on making the weekly variance Excel models more dynamic and automated so it takes only thirty minutes a week. ✗ • **Build product knowledge**—Build a deep understanding of the drivers of the business and how they change by attending FB courses (BizCamp) and finding the right points of contact (POCs) to meet with. Read through and review all relevant top-line communications, including H1/H2 docs, the monthly FB App doc, and FAST monthly reviews, and ask questions when things don't make sense. This will enable me to find opportunities to provide impact to my business partners. ✔
Personal	N/A	• Read three books. ✔ • Send a V4 level in bouldering. ✔ • Teach my dog how to roll over. ✔

You'll notice that I included personal goals in this template I shared with my manager. This was hugely beneficial because once my manager was on board with these goals, he and I carved out time for me to hit them. I might normally prioritize work over achieving these personal goals, but this meant I could give them the importance they deserved. For example, I would go to the bouldering gym on Tuesdays and Thursdays, so we made sure I was done with meetings by 5:00 p.m. on those days.

Similarly, at Google we set goals every six months. However, they're called OKRs (objectives and key results). We set them at the team level and individual level. Below is an example of my OKRs for my first half year at Google. You'll notice that we prioritize with P0, P1, and P2 markings. P0 means high priority, P1 is second priority, and P2 includes nice-to-haves.

Setting these goals will make it easier to track how close you are to achieving them by the end of each half year. This will also make it easier to do performance reviews and check if you've met expectations or exceeded them.

Objective Type	Objective Category	Amy's Key Results	P0/ P1	% of Time
Team	Create a positive culture for team members	• Help organize and attend team related events (e.g., virtual team lunches, off-site planning).	P1	5%
Work	Ramp up	• Become the go-to analyst for 3P. • Take time to invest in learning (e.g., Analytics Academy "Confidently Navigate Your Role as an Analyst" course, "GCS Ads Data structure" course).	P0	25%
	Develop opportunity sizing for lead generation and lead sharing pilot	• Develop opportunity sizing for the lead generation pilot proposal.	P0	25%
	Analyze GTM options for churn coupons	• Develop opportunity sizing for the churn pilot proposal. • Get alignment from XFN partners on churn coupon roadmap.	P0	25%
	Reporting on pilot KPIs and setting up incrementality measurement details	• Run analyses to deep dive on relevant trends before the revenue review call if necessary. • Leverage these insights into ongoing/new projects.	P1	10%
Personal	Personal improvement	• Bake three new recipes. • Learn five new songs on the ukulele.	P1	10%

Dealing with Imposter Syndrome

It's totally natural to feel imposter syndrome at work. For example, when my Facebook recruiter reached out to me saying that I got the job, I was thinking, "They must have made some mistake." But that's not true! I passed the interview process and I belonged at the company. The problem is confidence in your own abilities and potential. I've outlined a few steps that might help you overcome these initial feelings.

First, recognize when you feel like a fraud. For example, if you're one of the first or few women or a minority in your field or workplace, it's only natural that you sometimes feel like you don't totally fit in. Rather than taking your self-doubt as a sign of your ineptness, realize that it may just be a normal response to being an outsider.

Second, write a new script in your mind. In certain situations that trigger imposter feelings (e.g., starting a new job or project), instead of thinking, "Wait until they find out I have no idea what I'm doing," start by telling yourself, "Everyone new feels off-base at the beginning, and it takes time to ramp up. While I don't know all the answers now, I'm smart enough to figure them out."

Even Sheryl Sandberg, who has occupied high-level positions at Google and Meta, disclosed her personal failings and feelings of self-doubt in her book *Lean In: Women, Work, and the Will to Lead.* Although this book is controversial at certain points, I would still recommend it, as it has a core message of urging women to envision more in their professional lives. It's comforting to know that even individuals like Sandberg, who appear highly competent on the outside, also experience the same sense of imposter syndrome. Sometimes it just helps to hear that you're not alone.

In *Lean In*, Sandberg writes, "In order to continue to grow and challenge myself, I have to believe in my own abilities. I still face situations that I fear are beyond my capabilities. I still have days when I feel like a fraud. And I still sometimes find myself spoken over and discounted while men sitting next to me are not. But now I know how to take a deep breath and keep my hand up. I have learned to sit at the table."[42]

Networking In-House

Don't wait to be invited to meet people! In your first three or four weeks, prioritize getting to know people and make sure to set up virtual or in-person meetings with your team members. Create a list of the key people that you want to talk to and schedule 1:1s. This could be two per day or two per week, depending on your time and geographical constraints. Remember—1:1s are the most valuable activity you can focus on when ramping up!

For every 1:1, try to get to know the person as well as the role. For example, you can consider asking these questions:

- What are you working on?
- What does your life look like? (e.g., Have you moved recently? Do you have family nearby? Do you have any hobbies? What are your weekend activities? Are there any fun facts I should know about you?)
- Whom else should I get to know or talk to?
- Where can I get better connected in the company and team? (e.g., affinity groups, happy hours, mailing lists)

Once you've had a chance to understand the team, decide whom you would like to have a regular 1:1 with (and schedule it in your calendar).

---

42 Sheryl Sandberg, *Lean In: Women, Work, and the Will to Lead* (New York: Alfred A. Knopf, 2013), 38.

Last, don't be afraid to meet with leaders who have a much higher title and rank. At Facebook, there were monthly "office hours" with the VPs of finance (and similar but quarterly office hours at Google). I ended up taking advantage of that time. By getting to know the leaders, I started to understand a little more about how an executive thinks and what's at the forefront of their minds.

Giving and Receiving Feedback

Giving and receiving feedback is a critical part of your own growth and will help you to both succeed in your role and learn to be a leader. However, it can be hard to get up the courage to give feedback to others or to learn to do it in a way that's constructive and sensitive. Receiving feedback, on the other hand, can be anxiety inducing and sometimes a tough pill to swallow, and it takes practice to use it to your advantage. Below are some useful tips that will help you to navigate this process.

Giving Feedback

Make it timely.

Feedback is more relevant when it's provided close to when the event or behavior occurred. The context is still fresh in everyone's mind, and they have the opportunity to make improvements immediately rather than waiting until their next performance review.

Make it specific and actionable.

Providing specifics and clear next steps is the best way to make feedback actionable. When giving feedback, spend at least as much time looking forward (e.g., "In case you find it helpful, here are three things you can consider trying next time . . .") as you spend looking back (e.g., "I noticed in our meeting last week, and again yesterday, that you did X, which comes across to others as . . ."). If you're having a hard time coming up with specific suggestions, offer to brainstorm with the feedback recipient.

Balance the constructive with the positive and build trust.

Our minds vividly remember "constructive" feedback (when we're asked to change) much more than "positive" feedback (when we're told we're doing the right thing and to keep it up). Constructive feedback is essential for growth, but positive feedback is energizing and motivating, so striking the right balance can help others feel encouraged to make changes for improvement. Noticing what's going well also shows others that you're paying attention and that you care. This builds a foundation of credibility and trust—"Hey, this is a person who notices what I do"—and that foundation will make it easier to bring up a "constructive" piece of feedback. Also, if you give more feedback more often, I bet you'll notice more things to appreciate than to improve over time, and this regular "boost" will take the sting out of any constructive criticism.

Include ideas that help them go from "great" to "amazing."

At tech companies, we think about bugs and feature requests—it's how we make our products better. Bugs are problems that need solving, and feature requests are new opportunities to make a product even better than it already is. What if we applied the same thinking to our feedback conversations to make each other the best we can be? Giving feedback is often like "filing a bug." We notice a flaw or someone not doing what we think they should be doing, and that's the end of the conversation. By working "feature requests" into our conversations as well, we can help (already great) coworkers take their performance to the next level and surprise and delight their peers, managers, and clients. For example, "I noticed that you're very proficient with analytical tools like Excel, and I always appreciate when you're able to take on a portion of the analysis. One quick feature request for the future, though—I have noticed that you tend to rely on other analysts for SQL pulls, and I think this is an area that we can work together to improve on!" Take the opportunity to help your peers or direct reports stretch and grow.

Handle tough feedback with care.

Some feedback can be tough to hear. This might be when:

- the feedback is about someone's personality or working style.
- it's more negative than expected or does not reflect the full context of the situation.
- it doesn't clearly articulate the problem.
- the receiver does not agree with it.

The next time you're facing a situation in which you need to deliver tough feedback, take some time to reflect on who you're giving the feedback to, how you'll involve them in the conversation, and how you'll frame it. Consider these tips as you prepare:

Say this:	Instead of this:	Feedback principle
"You have such creative ideas. Let's brainstorm ways to ensure your perspective is heard more in team discussions."	"You're too shy. Speak up more in team meetings."	Make it about the individual's behaviors rather than their personality.

Say this:	Instead of this:	Feedback principle
"I think you're being perceived as someone who doesn't care . . ."	"You don't care."	Highlight how the individual's behavior is being perceived, especially if you anticipate the behavior may not reflect their intentions.
"I felt disrespected when I wasn't able to finish my thought completely."	"You constantly interrupted me."	Share the impact of the behavior—how did it make you feel and why?—rather than just stating the behavior. It's more difficult for people to argue with how you were made to feel, and sharing the impact can help motivate behavior change.
"The client complained that X . . . Is there any additional context I should know?"	"The client complained that X . . . You didn't think about their needs."	Consider the possibility that the feedback recipient may have additional facts or context that would impact your assessment of the situation. Whenever appropriate, take their perspective into account.

Say this:	Instead of this:	Feedback principle
"One thing you might consider is jotting down your thoughts as they come to you so you don't forget them and then waiting for an appropriate pause in the conversation where you can share your thoughts."	"You seem really scattered."	Give specific suggestions for next steps rather than focusing on the problem.
"What are your thoughts?" or "Help me understand . . ."	"Why did you do that?" or "Didn't you know she had already made that decision?"	Ask open-ended questions to make sure the recipient understands what you're saying.

Receiving Feedback

It can be difficult to graciously accept constructive criticism. The moment you hear the word "feedback," your heartbeat may quicken and your mind begins to race. Know that you're not alone. Unfortunately, in the heat of the moment, many of us react with defensiveness and anger. But the truth is, we need to get over it. There's value in constructive criticism! How else would we identify weaknesses that can help us maintain relationships and be more successful in everything we do?

Here's a seven-step process to help you better handle constructive criticism from your manager or a peer:

1. Pause your initial reaction and listen.

My initial reaction after hearing criticism is to immediately talk back and defend myself. But before you do that, try listening to what the other person has to say, and hold back your reaction to interrupt. Do not let your emotions and ego get in the way of progress! Keep your eye contact and allow the speaker to finish their statements. Good listening is the first step to receiving feedback, and in doing so, you'll give your brain time to process the information.

2. Remember the benefits of feedback.

Even the best employees can benefit from feedback. These are the types of people who are typically not challenged as much as they should be and could become complacent. Therefore, it would behoove these star employees (like you!) to know what to do to further improve work relationships and skills.

Nobody likes to admit failure, but at the same time, nobody is perfect! If you keep a growth mindset and focus more on your ability to change and grow, then you will be able to see feedback as an opportunity for improvement. This will allow you to dream bigger and set new goals that stretch your limits!

3. Make sure to take notes.

In the heat of the moment, you may have a lot of emotions, and it can be hard to keep track of all the details. In order to make sure you don't forget these golden nuggets of information, repeat back what they've said and then take notes. For example, "Just to reiterate and make sure I understand—I hear you saying that you want me to loop you into all stakeholder emails in the future. Is that correct?" Summarizing the takeaways in your own words will help to solidify your understanding and allow the other person to clarify if needed.

Taking down these notes helps you facilitate further conversations. You can check in every month with your manager to review progress and set goals based on prior feedback. To address some of the previous feedback notes, I would say something like, "I've gotten feedback before that I was excluding the team on stakeholder communications in the past. I understand this caused confusion and some duplication of efforts. Do you think I'm making improvements on this front? Is there anything else I could improve on?" It can be gratifying to find out that you're making steps forward and chipping away at your goal.

4. Say thank you.

Take time to show gratitude to the person who is sharing feedback with you. You can say something along these lines: "I appreciate you sharing this feedback with me. I understand these conversations can be difficult, but I know they're critical to my professional development. I'll work on X." You don't necessarily have to agree with their point of view, but at least you're acknowledging their thoughts.

Assume positive intent. Whoever is giving feedback is likely genuinely trying to help you improve. They see your potential and want to help you harness and nurture your gifts.

5. Ask questions to deconstruct the feedback.

Now that you've taken a pause to listen and process the feedback, now is your time to ask clarifying questions. Although it can be tempting, don't hurry through the conversation just to get it over.

If your manager is telling you that you could improve on structuring the meetings that you lead, you could have the following conversation.

> You: "Thank you so much for letting me know that. Would you mind sharing a specific example of this so I can improve in the future?"
>
> Manager: "No problem at all. During the weekly business review yesterday, Mike asked a question and the entire

conversation got derailed. We ran out of time before going through the critical next steps slide."

You: "Yes, you're right that we went down a rabbit hole and ran out of time for the slides we wanted to get through. How do you suggest I handle this differently in the future?"

Manager: "I suggest sending out an agenda ahead of time in an email. Run through the agenda at the beginning of the meeting so that all stakeholders are aware of the direction the conversation is going. If needed, steer the conversation back to the topic at hand. This way, we can cover all the important items in a structured manner."

You: "Thank you for clarifying! From now on, I will make sure to create and share an agenda before my meetings."

In this example conversation, you gracefully received your manager's feedback and asked for clarity, and now you can more easily take action on the feedback given.

6. Request follow-up time if needed.

In an ideal scenario, you would be able to come to an agreement on next steps, but obviously, navigating these feedback conversations is not easy. It's totally okay to take time to process the feedback and then request a follow-up meeting to ask more questions and align on next steps.

For me, it's helpful to document my feedback as soon as I receive it so I don't forget any valuable piece of information. Some sample feedback notes follow. In addition, after leadership review meetings, I try to generalize some of the feedback I've had so that it's more applicable for me in the future. This also helps me develop my executive presence and thinking skills.

Amy's Sample Feedback Document

- When presenting to senior audiences, think bigger picture (e.g., don't walk them through the entire equation in detail).
- Make sure to leave space between slides for questions.
- Before answering, listen to the entire question first before forming a response.
- Tag stakeholders into the document before the presentation, in order to get early feedback.

7. Schedule regular feedback sessions going forward.

I personally prefer inviting feedback often and consistently rather than all at once. I'd rather know how to meet and exceed expectations of my managers and peers, rather than be caught off-guard by negative feedback during a performance review cycle. By setting up specific time on the calendar for feedback, you can regularly evaluate yourself and figure out how to make adjustments in order to achieve your goals.

Finally, don't forget to get feedback from a variety of sources. This is also known as 360 feedback. Ask peers, managers, and direct reports for their perspectives so you can get well-rounded insights. For example, your manager would be able to give more relevant comments on your executive presence, while your direct reports would be able to better comment on your management style and mentorship.

Securing Promotions

Depending on your ambitions, you may be ready to move on from the fun of the honeymoon period and want to get promoted between one and four years after securing your new role. At that point, pick your project and boss very carefully. It takes about two years on a team to get to a level of high enough productivity to secure a promotion. Typically, people switch teams right after a promotion. Switching at any other time would set your productivity and timeline to the next promotion back.

At Google, the promotion process is done by committee. Twice a year, you have the option to check a box to request a promotion. You'll pick the reviewers, including peers and your boss. Then, the promotion committee will review all the packets in one long day and make sure your rating is calibrated. You can even get promoted against the will of your boss, so you should always consider applying for a promotion if you want it, even if your manager is not supportive (this is more unlikely at Meta).

These are some useful tips that will help you to improve your chances of securing a promotion when the time comes:

Documenting Your Work

In order to help you hit your promotion, one tip I've heard is that you should keep a private document about what you're working on and visit it a few times a week. Documenting your work frequently will provide you with a reference you can bring to your performance review, will help you identify patterns in your work and places you're hitting roadblocks, and will highlight areas where you spend most of your time, revealing your strengths and interests.[43]

43 Corey Kosak, comment on "What Are Some Useful Tips for Someone Who Is Starting Work at Google?" Quora, last modified June 24, 2017, https://www.quora.com/What-are-some-useful-tips-for-someone-who-is-starting-work-at-Google.

Giving Thanks

It's always good to show appreciation to your coworkers for a job well done, especially if they go above and beyond. At Google and Meta, there are systems in place for officially recognizing others, and these recognitions from peers are taken into account during the performance review cycles. This means that you could be helping your coworker secure that promotion! Also, I've found that the more you're appreciative of others, the more likely others will reciprocate.

At Google, there are two ways to give thanks:

Kudos: There is a system of sending kudos to peers for helping or doing a great job. The manager of the colleague is copied in on it so the company is made aware of your accomplishments, and this could help you with your performance review.

Peer bonuses: You can send a colleague a nice little bonus if they've done something beyond their call of duty (you have five opportunities each quarter to do this). This program allows peers to reward an activity that could have gone completely unnoticed by managers. The colleague's manager has to sign off on it, so it can't be completely frivolous. I like maxing out on these because it doesn't cost you anything, but it makes the other person feel great. They get to take their family for a nice dinner. Plus, a lot of people brag about peer bonuses on their perf (Google's performance review system).

At Meta, there's one way to give thanks:

Thanks Bot: Thanks Bot is a tool that helps to cultivate an attitude of gratitude at Meta and is similar to Kudos at Google. Employees can write "#thanks @Amy Yan for helping me on project X."

Once you send the #thanks, the person you thanked and their manager will receive an email with your note, and the #thanks will be sent to the Meta performance tool, where it will be added to their feedback history.

Most managers do take this into account for performance review cycles, so it's important that you take advantage of these tools!

Changing Careers or Transitioning Roles

You may have gotten to the point when you *should* be considering promotion, but you've found that your current career is not the right fit for you. This is not a failure—it's an opportunity to try an exciting new field or industry. So, how should you handle looking for a career change?

There are two parts to making a career change. The first part is getting to know yourself: your values, interests, and what lights you up. You need to know what you're passionate about so you can pursue this in your new career. If that feels hard to answer, one way of gathering data on yourself is noticing your "energy breadcrumbs"—that is, what are the topics that you can spend hours on and not realize the time has passed? What do you seem to show up to, no matter what your mood is?

The second part of this equation is getting over your fears and "What if?" thoughts around a career change and making the leap wholeheartedly. Both parts will be an ongoing journey.

If you're having trouble figuring out your next step, try reading Richard Bolles and Katharine Brooks's book *What Color Is Your Parachute?* on life purpose. It includes great questions to help you decide what you want to do with your life.

The good news is that your role has prepared you for many different career paths. As a BizOps analyst, you'll have the skills to easily transition to other roles, like product management, product marketing management, program management, or data science!

As with any type of transition, it's easiest to change *either* your role *or* the company rather than both. For example, if you work in the BizOps team at Meta, it's easier to transition to a product manager position at Meta than one at Google.

To make a lateral transition internally, start by searching the internal job postings. The internal transfer process at both Google and Meta is pretty straightforward. You'll need one year of experience in your current role, manager approval, and one or two cycles of ratings that are at least "meets expectations."

There is plenty that you can do to prepare yourself and the team you're interested in transitioning to. Let's say you're interested in product management. Reach out to current PMs to shadow them or get more involved with that type of work. Since the BizOps role is so collaborative, you'll likely have already interacted with these types of teams and know what their day-to-day responsibilities are. Ask for advice around preparing for the role and interview, and do mock interviews with current PMs before applying.

Closing Thoughts

CONGRATULATIONS ON MAKING IT through the entire book!

You now understand the business operations role in tech and what your day-to-day would be like in companies like Google and Meta. You know how to prepare for that role, develop contacts and network, and apply for job openings. Most importantly, you know exactly what to expect in interviews, including what types of questions the interviewers will ask, what they're looking for, and what strategies to use to stand out. Finally, you know how to succeed in that role once it's yours and start building a prestigious career.

The next step is to practice all these strategies and techniques you've learned. What separates you from other candidates will be the amount of time you invest! Preparing for interviews takes a lot of time and effort, but trust me—the investment is worth it to land a fulfilling job.

You have all the information you need to succeed. Reading this book has already made you more prepared than the average applicant. Now, the rest of the work is up to you. Wishing you the best of luck!

Q and A with Craig Fenton, Director of Strategy and Operations at Google

THIS IS A BONUS chapter in which you and I get the chance to interview a successful director in the BizOps realm. This is a valuable opportunity to hear firsthand from a director about what it takes to thrive in strategy, the personality traits and strengths that lend themselves to this career path, and how to forge a career path when you're just getting started.

Craig Fenton is a business leader and entrepreneur who has worked in the technology industry for twenty years. He leads strategy and operations for Google in the UK and Ireland, is an investor in and mentor of several startups, and founded his own record label to give young artists from lower socioeconomic areas their start in music.

Craig has a podcast and YouTube channel called *Coffee, Eggs & Inspiration* where he interviews inspiring leaders about their story. Craig lives with his family in London and has been there for twenty years and counting.

Amy Yan: Tell me a little about yourself and your background as the Strategy and Operations Director for Google.

Craig Fenton: My role title is Strategy and Operations Director, and it's a combination of the COO and CSO roles. On the "strategy" piece, we write the business plan once a year and examine where we see company growth. Then we determine how we want to organize ourselves to address that growth, what the competitive landscape looks like, and what the external forces look like. The "operations" part of it is organizing the business and operating it, ranging from defining the OKRs (how we measure success and the metrics that matter), making headcount decisions and other investment decisions, and looking at skills and the anatomy of the human resources we have. Do we have the right people in the right places for the movement of the business?

AY: How did you decide to go into business operations?

CF: My role before Google was at Accenture and I was in sales; I led a sales team in the EMEA region. I've always been more interested in the strategy side—understanding market context and defining the path through it. I think the smart thing we do at Google is we bring the strategy together with operations. So, it's not good enough just to have smart and interesting ideas—you need to be able to execute them. There's no point in having a brilliant strategy that doesn't get done. For me, the operational inclusion is super interesting; you get to set the direction and then execute it.

AY: What makes you excited to go into work every morning?

CF: I thrive on variety. I love to be a little bit uncomfortable all the time ("comfortably uncomfortable"). I like changing things and building things. Because it feels like whether you're changing it or building it, you're moving something and creating impact in a way that's hopefully valuable and matters.

Like most, I'm energized by the people I work with, and I love my team and get energy from them. Particularly, I enjoy being challenged to think in different ways by people who look at facts with a different set of eyes because of their backgrounds and experiences. I really love that.

I have a bunch of hobbies or side hustles outside of work, and that gives me energy. For me, that's balance as well. My wife calls me an active relaxer.

AY: Why did you choose Google particularly? I know you mentioned the people, but is there anything else?

CF: Yes, a couple of reasons. I'm a bit of a gadget geek. Although I don't code, I understand technology and, more importantly, its implications in a business or human context. This dates back to when I was a child, tinkering around in the shed with my grandfather and building circuits and trolleys and mechanical items. I like technology, and Google is one of a few things that epitomize that domain and are moving the world.

On the personal side, I grew up in New Zealand, and it was a country of three million people. You had to sit on an aircraft for eight hours to reach a country other than Australia. The first exotic stop was Indonesia! I grew up pre-internet in the early stage of my professional career, before Larry and Sergey started building their servers in a garage in Mountain View. Everything that we currently do in our day-to-day job was completely unimaginable at that time. I found the thought of big business and what was happening "overseas" absolutely exotic, intoxicating, and slightly unreachable.

The wonderful thing about Google is that it has democratized and flattened the world. The platforms that we have are enabling people with great ideas and a smartphone to reach a global audience. We've made sure people's voices are heard on important topics in an unedited and uncensored way. As a guy who grew up in isolated New Zealand, a country obscurely positioned at the bottom of the world, this is all like magic to me still.

AY: What professional advice would you give your younger self?

CF: Follow your passion! I think that's the answer that most people would give. Take the time to get to know yourself. It sounds strange, but a lot of us are too busy living life to reflect inwardly on what excites us. I think it's really important to get a sense of that and follow that passion.

The signs of something that excites you are easy to spot. You tend to light up, your eyes get brighter, you talk quicker, you become engaged, you devour books on the topic, watch YouTube or other sources to learn more, and spend all your spare time on the topic. These are all signs that you're really interested in something.

Follow your passion, and don't be afraid to take risks, and in fact, embrace them and seek them out. It's when you take the biggest risks that you make the biggest movements in personal well-being and happiness.

AY: Outside of passion, what kind of skills, abilities, and personal attributes do you think are essential for success in this role?

CF: Well, we're in an ever-changing world. I think the answer to that question today is different than what it would have been when I was coming out of university. In a changing world, the reality is that we're preparing for jobs that don't exist, for companies that haven't been founded, using technology that hasn't been invented. The half-life of companies is shortening; the only constant thing is change, and that's the only predictable thing as well. In that context, your ability to remain adaptable, to thrive and seek ambiguity, and to have a continuous learning mindset (because most of the things we see these days are not what we've seen before) are essential. Imagine a future different than today and then go create it. These are different ways to describe creativity.

The singular answer above all else is a curiosity-driven skill in creativity. Use that wonderful human capacity of imagination in a valuable way to think about the world around you and to come up with surprising ideas. Whether that's getting that side of the brain working with music, art, dance, or doing it in the context that we do it. We call creativity in business "innovation." I think that's the most important skill.

You also need to be able to communicate and have great interpersonal skills, but these are just table stakes. They're necessary but insufficient.

AY: Did you always know you wanted to be a people manager, or did you ever consider the individual contributor route?

CF: I didn't really know what a people manager was, and I still don't think it's really a thing. All of us, to a greater extent, are social animals. That's why we live in communities and groups. Actually, in the animal kingdom, humans are unique in that they live in very big groups.

When I was young, my father always encouraged me to play team sports. I suppose that's the earliest example of operating in a collective toward a shared goal. I always loved the feeling of being part of a team, to be working collectively toward a shared objective, and to get to know each other so well that you anticipate what's going to happen next and what that person can and will do.

That's the thrill of people management. I don't see it as a hierarchical thing at all. I think of all of us as individual contributors, including myself, Sundar Pichai, and the president of the United States. They're also leaders in the service of a collective that is operating toward a shared objective. That's the thrill of what we call "people management," but that term is a rather transactional way of describing it. For me, it's a form of teamwork and leadership.

AY: What are the next steps for you? Would you be interested in transitioning to another role?

CF: Never say never. I made a point to follow this personal rule of not spending longer than two to three years in a single role.

That doesn't mean changing companies, but it means expanding or changing my role in some ways.

For me, I really love strategy. I like building things and changing things, like applications or companies. I'm an angel investor, so I love working with young entrepreneurs. I have a record label—that keeps me interested and busy. So, I would never say never; I will always seek change and renewal. It could be an expanded version of what I'm doing at the moment, whether that's covering more and different countries or units of the business, transitioning to a different part of Google, or even transitioning outside the company if it takes my fancy!

AY: How did you start getting involved with angel investing?

CF: I guess I've always had the entrepreneurial gene since my father was an entrepreneur. I watched him build up a business, crash it, and then rebuild it. I've always found that really interesting. At the same time, my career has taken me mostly in corporate, paid-for and salaried roles. Angel investing is a great way of exercising that entrepreneurial spirit through the agency of others (young or old entrepreneurs). Investing in people's ideas and working with them on those ideas is a great way of expressing that interest.

So far, for me, I've got a portfolio of nine companies now that I've invested in. They're pretty different. They're in different places, ranging from New Zealand to Kenya to the UK and the US. They're all in different industries, from fintech, to health, to music, but they all have technology at their hearts. I try to stick with what I know and I kind of know technology. So, if something comes to me that's related to real estate or food, I typically won't invest in it because I don't feel I understand it well enough.

AY: What do you enjoy doing outside of work?

CF: I fly planes! I'm a pilot and I've got a small plane that I fly. I took it to Scotland the other day. I like to spend time with my family and go on long walks. I've got two teenage boys, eighteen and fifteen. I like spending time with them, but I'm not sure the reverse is true anymore. As much as I can, I love to travel. I love the culture, food, and history while visiting places. Last, I've got these businesses outside of work that I consider my passion and hustle.

Annotated Further Resources

For more job search tips and resources, see:

- http://www.wonsulting.com/
- hello@wonsulting.com

For a more in-depth discussion of maximizing your career, see:

- Karen, Alana. *The Adventures of Women in Tech: How We Got Here and Why We Stay.* Minneapolis, MN: Wise Ink Creative Publishing, 2020.
- Sandberg, Sheryl, and Nell Scovell. *Lean In: Women, Work, and the Will to Lead.* New York: Alfred A. Knopf, 2013.

For a more in-depth discussion of career exploration and preparing for a job, see:

- Bolles, Richard Nelson, and Katharine Brooks. *What Color Is Your Parachute? 2021: A Practical Manual for Job-Hunters and Career-Changers.* Berkeley, CA: Ten Speed Press, 2020.

For a more in-depth discussion of technology and business strategy, see:

- Detroja, Parth, Aditya Agashe, and Neel Mehta. *Swipe to Unlock: The Primer on Technology and Business Strategy.* Self-published, CreateSpace, 2017.

For a more in-depth discussion of automating tasks using Python, see:

- Sweigart, Al. *Automate the Boring Stuff with Python: Practical Programming for Total Beginners.* San Francisco, CA: No Starch Press, 2015.

For a more in-depth discussion of case interview preparation, see:

- Cosentino, Marc. *Case In Point: Complete Case Interview Preparation.* 8th ed. Santa Barbara, CA: Burgee Press, 2013.

For a more in-depth discussion of facing adversity, building resilience, and finding joy, see:

- Sandberg, Sheryl, and Adam M. Grant. *Option B: Facing Adversity, Building Resilience, and Finding Joy.* New York: Alfred A. Knopf, 2017.

For more information and resources, please visit amysunyan.com!